"Like the best words always are, 'apprentice' is rooted in the generations before us, making sense of the way we learn. At its heart it is about binding oneself to someone who knows more. In reading Matthew Dickerson we are drawn into his long apprenticeship to J. R. R. Tolkien, the master story-teller whose moral imagination shapes every soul who enters into his world of hobbits and their ways. But the thread that weaves this tale is about learning to learn to follow Jesus—not the pursuit of the power of a ring—and therefore a pilgrimage in the imitation of Christ, of binding ourselves to the truest truths of the universe."

—**Steven Garber**
Professor of Marketplace Theology, Regent College;
author of *Visions of Vocation: Common Grace for the Common Good*

"Matt Dickerson reminds us that Jesus didn't tell us just to win souls or get people to accept Jesus into their hearts; Jesus told disciples to make disciples. What is so good about Matt's book is that he takes that imperative and turns it over and over to unpack the relationality it entails, the necessity of knowing and living the word it requires, and the temptations of a culture that clouds our discernment and threatens to undermine our calling as disciple-makers. The book is an engaging conversation that humbly helps get us back on track to do the most significant thing that Christ called us to do."

—**Dennis Okholm**
Author of *Monk Habits for Everyday People*

"In a world of Insta-discipleship and Bible study by 140 characters, Professor Matthew Dickerson calls us to a different way. When it comes to making disciples, one size does not fit all. *Disciple Making in a Culture of Power, Comfort, and Fear* is a great book which challenged me to love Jesus more and to look at the opportunities around me to point others toward him."

—**Kevin A. Thompson**
Pastor, Community Bible Church, Fort Smith, Arkansas

"From Dallas Willard to Eugene Peterson, many fine writers have tackled the subject of Christian discipleship. Few, however, have produced such a fun read. Matt Dickerson combines the practical and the personal in a way that is both remarkably edifying and utterly delightful."

—**Paula Huston**
Author of *A Land Without Sin*

"Matt Dickerson's work brings to the forefront that disciples must be truly formed by Christ to be disciple-makers. Matt's cultural analysis, precise exegesis, while plumbing the writings of Christian saints, coupled with his own journey, unfolds a depth of timeless orthodoxy. Matt Dickerson leads us from cultural conformity, and the solely cognitive, to the soul forming work of Word, words, and Spirit. From this well, disciples and disciple-makers are born. I cannot help recommend this work to all who desire to reach higher and deeper."

—**Dale Edwards**
Regional Executive Minister, American Baptist Churches
of Vermont and New Hampshire

Disciple Making in a Culture of Power, Comfort, and Fear

Disciple Making in a Culture of Power, Comfort, and Fear

MATTHEW DICKERSON

CASCADE *Books* • Eugene, Oregon

DISCIPLE MAKING IN A CULTURE OF POWER, COMFORT, AND FEAR

Copyright © 2020 Matthew Dickerson. All rights reserved. Except for brief quotations in critical publications or reviews, no part of this book may be reproduced in any manner without prior written permission from the publisher. Write: Permissions, Wipf and Stock Publishers, 199 W. 8th Ave., Suite 3, Eugene, OR 97401.

Cascade Books
An Imprint of Wipf and Stock Publishers
199 W. 8th Ave., Suite 3
Eugene, OR 97401

www.wipfandstock.com

PAPERBACK ISBN: 978-1-7252-5493-0
HARDCOVER ISBN: 978-1-7252-5494-7
EBOOK ISBN: 978-1-7252-5495-4

Scripture quotations marked (NIV) are taken from the Holy Bible, New International Version®, NIV®. Copyright © 1973, 1978, 1984, 2011 by Biblica, Inc.™ Used by permission of Zondervan. All rights reserved worldwide. www.zondervan.com The "NIV" and "New International Version" are trademarks registered in the United States Patent and Trademark Office by Biblica, Inc.™

Where indicated, Scripture quotations are from THE MESSAGE, copyright © 1993, 2002, 2018 by Eugene H. Peterson. Used by permission of NavPress. All rights reserved. Represented by Tyndale House Publishers, Inc.

Where indicated, Scripture quotations are taken from Revised Standard Version of the Bible, copyright © 1946, 1952, and 1971 National Council of the Churches of Christ in the United States of America. Used by permission. All rights reserved worldwide.

Cataloguing-in-Publication data:

Names: Dickerson, Matthew, author.
Title: Disciple making in a culture of power, comfort, and fear / Matthew Dickerson.
Description: Eugene, OR: Cascade Books, 2020 | Includes bibliographical references and index.
Identifiers: ISBN 978-1-7252-5493-0 (paperback) | ISBN 978-1-7252-5494-7 (hardcover) | ISBN 978-1-7252-5495-4 (ebook)
Subjects: LCSH: Spiritual life—Christianity. | Christian life.
Classification: BV4501.3 2020 (print) | BV4501.3 (ebook)

Manufactured in the U.S.A. JUNE 5, 2020

In memory of Eugene and Janice Peterson.

The devil's temptation strategy is to depersonalize the ways of Jesus but leave the way itself intact. His strategy is the same with us. But a way that is depersonalized, carried out without love or intimacy or participation, is not, no matter how well we do it, no matter how much good is accomplished, the Jesus way … The devil is the consummate ideologue, but he is incapable of incarnation. He uses people to embody his projects in functional rather than personal relationships. The devil is the ultimate in disincarnation. Every time that we embrace ways other than the ways of Jesus, try to manipulate people or events in ways that short-circuit personal relationships and intimacies, we are doing the devil's work.

—Eugene Peterson, *The Jesus Way*.

Contents

Acknowledgments | ix

Introduction | xi

1 Disciples as Disciple Makers (and the Importance of Lenses) | 1
2 Disciple Making and the Word of God | 14
3 Disciple Making and Relationship | 31
4 Disciple Making and Christian Community | 44
5 Three Metaphors for Disciple Making | 56
6 The Lust of the Eyes and Flesh:
   A Threefold Look at Temptation, Part I | 71
7 Pride of Life: A Threefold Look at Temptation, Part II | 92
8 A Short Conclusion:
   "But What Do I Actually Do To Make Disciples?" | 110

Bibliography | 125

Acknowledgments

THANKS TO NATHAN FOSTER, Paula Huston, and Kevin Thompson for helpful comments on my first drafts; to Stephanie Allen for half a decade (and counting) of challenging, insightful, enjoyable teaching that has informed this book (even if I didn't quote her); to my Memorial Baptist Church (Middlebury, Vermont) and Chrysostom Society families for fellowship, support, and encouragement; and to my wife Deborah for years of joyful co-labor in disciple making.

I'm grateful to numerous authors, speakers, and thinkers—theologians, pastors, and writers on spiritual formation as well as poets and novelists—whose books have helped shaped my thinking. Some who have profoundly influenced me primarily through their writings include: C. S. Lewis, N. T. Wright, Steven Garber, J. R. R. Tolkien, John Stott, John White, Wendell Berry, and Francis Schaeffer. In a few cases I've been especially fortunate to have personally met—and witnessed the lives and examples of—faithful followers of Christ who may have taught me not only through their writing or teaching (though they have often done that in profound ways), but who also influenced me through their lives: Christ-followers who spoke to me through their lives what they also spoke to me in words: Doug Dean, Dick Keyes, Stephanie Allen, J. P. Moreland, Richard Foster, Eugene Peterson, Walter Wangerin, Jr., Paula Huston, Tom Howard, Peter Kreeft, Luci Shaw, and Norman Wirzba, and especially my good friend David O'Hara and my wife Deborah. This book bears the fingerprints of all of these disciple makers.

Introduction

It was the worst moment of my life. The worst day. The worst week. The worst month.

The call came in a little before 7 AM east coast time—just 3 AM Alaska time—on an early January day. My brother's voice was shaky. His words few. He could barely bring himself to speak them before he hung up the phone. His son Brad, my nephew, a few weeks shy of his thirty-first birthday, had just been killed in a car accident in his home city of Anchorage.

The news was surreal and hard to fathom. I kept hoping to wake up and find it out it had been a nightmare, or a mistake. How could this happen? How could this happen *to Brad*? How could this happen to my brother and his family? What do we do now? How do we go on?

A few details were known. Others emerged slowly over the next few months. Brad had gone on a short errand to the grocery store a couple of miles from his house, and was heading back home, driving past our favorite Anchorage coffee shop, just a few hundred yards from turning off the busy four-lane road onto the relative safety of his quiet side street. Another car going in the opposite direction swerved all the way across the highway straight into oncoming traffic, hitting my nephew head-on and killing both drivers instantly. As we would later learn, the other driver had already sideswiped another car some distance back the road, and was fleeing from that accident. According to some witnesses, he had turned off his headlights, perhaps to avoid being followed. Brad, in his Subaru wagon, was traveling behind a truck with a plow. The truck swerved out of the way just in time to avoid the oncoming vehicle, so Brad probably never saw it coming. When the toxicology report was released several months later, it confirmed what we had already guessed: the other driver was high on meth.

None of those details mattered much. When they came out, one by one, they couldn't have made the grief much worse than it already was any

Introduction

more than they could have brought any real comfort. Certainly they didn't matter at the time. Only one detail mattered. We had lost Brad. Suddenly a big emptiness took his place in the lives of his parents, his brother, the woman whom he planned to marry likely later that same year. In my life also. I wept for days.

Brad had gone to Middlebury College, where I teach. Since his family lived in Alaska at the time, and regular travel home was not feasible for him, he spent a lot of time at our house during those four years. We'd been close already, but we drew even closer then. After his graduation, when Brad was living in Anchorage, I visited Alaska almost every summer, and several autumns as well. We had all sorts of outdoor adventures together: fishing, sea-kayaking, day hikes into the local passes, longer backpacking and camping trips, berry-picking excursions, and also explorations of local restaurants, ice cream shops, and cafes. But it wasn't my own loss I thought of most during those weeks and months; it was the loss suffered by my brother and sister-in-law, Ted and Susie; by my nephew Michael, Brad's brother; and by Ivy, his long-time girlfriend and the woman he had planned to marry, who'd felt like part of our family for years—who *was* part of our family.

As I pondered all that loss, many thoughts ran through my mind. The central thought was how unfair it seemed. My brother and sister-in-law were more than just faithful churchgoers; they had been active in church ministry all their lives, in small groups, and as youth leaders. Prior to his move to Alaska, Ted had served for years as an architect with an international missions agency, raising his own support and living on missionary wages. Ivy, in addition to being a delightful, kind, loving, fun young woman, was also very giving: a school teacher whose passion for helping kids had her working in one of the most challenging schools in the city. Michael had already had a year of hard setbacks with some of his life aspirations, and had been very close to Brad, sharing a house with him long after both had graduated from college. And Brad himself, in addition to being a creative, hard-working entrepreneur juggling three different start-up businesses, was one of the kindest and most generous thirty-year-old men I knew, always ready to help out those in need. My wife, Deborah, was especially fond of Brad, remembering his college-student days when he'd come over to our house *not* to play outdoors with his uncle and male cousins, sledding or shooting guns or chopping wood, but just to hang out with Deborah over

Introduction

a meal or cup of tea. How could this happen to that family? I asked that question repeatedly in the days that followed that horrible news.

And in pondering that question, I began to realize something about myself. Though I would never have articulated this as a belief—indeed, theologically speaking I would have argued strongly against it—I had come to *feel* that somehow because of the Christian faith of our family, of Ted's and Susie's family, that we could expect some amount of safety, protection, and even material gifts from God. Sure, I expected opposition to the gospel I believed in and sought to live by; I not only understood that as a Christian I would suffer some hardship and persecution for my faith, but I had experienced some of that opposition and hostility over the course of my life. And even if the opposition I experienced living in an affluent country with significant freedom of religion did not produce much in the way of *real* suffering, I knew that in many times and places around the world, Christians suffered tremendous persecution including imprisonment, torture, and death. I expected that to be a reality of our world, and to some extent accepted why God might allow it.

Yet when it came to the sort of unjust and seemingly random loss we had experienced with Brad's death as a result of a driver high on meth, deep down I expected *that* sort of suffering wouldn't hit our family. Even the passing of my mother six months before Brad hadn't hit me in the same way. My mother had died of cancer, which in some ways is every bit as random and meaningless as getting hit by a drunk or high driver. Except my mother lived into her mid-eighties, which in most moments of world history would have been considered an extraordinarily long life. Plus, when she'd been diagnosed with cancer, the doctor had said she might live five years with a constant regimen of chemotherapy; she'd gone on to survive twelve years! Though I grieved at the death of my mother and in many ways I still miss her, I could look at her situation and instead of complaining of the unfairness of her cancer, I could say that God had somehow blessed her (and all of her family) with more than double the life expectancy of a typical multiple myeloma patient. Maybe that was true. But I saw absolutely nothing in Brad's sudden death other than loss, tragedy, and unfairness. Nothing in it communicated to me any sort of blessing.

It still doesn't.

In modern parlance, though I didn't consciously or rationally *think* this, in some way I *felt* it: that as Christians we could expect some sort of

Introduction

"blessing" of health and wealth. Tragic deaths were things that happened to other people's families.

To be very clear: I believe this thinking is a lie. I did then. I do now. It is part of the so-called "prosperity gospel," which is not only bad theology, but also destructive. The prosperity gospel, sometimes called the "health-and-wealth gospel," teaches that those who have enough faith in God can expect God to provide them with extra material benefits, and also to protect them from harm, and heal all of their illnesses: a sort of reward system for faith: a quid pro quo. In short, it promises a life of comfort as a reward for faith—or, perhaps more to the point, a life of comfort in exchange for church attendance and financial giving. The propagandists of this false teaching often benefit greatly by calling their followers to prove their faith by contributing generously to the coffers controlled by none other than the propagandists themselves.

This teaching, however, is contrary to the teachings of the Bible. I had argued against the prosperity gospel for years. Yet I have also grown up in middle class America, of one of the most prosperous nations on earth. I have listened to countless advertisements telling me how I deserved this and that: a good job, a happy family, a nice car, a shampoo that made my hair shiny and luscious, a vacation, a good meal from McDonald's. I grew up in a nation far more enamored with rights than with responsibilities. The framers of our Constitution made a collection of these rights the first and most important addendums to their newly formed government. Anybody living in my country can make a long list of things we are supposed to have a right to: free education, free speech, a job, voting privileges, the bearing of arms, good health care, a fair trial. So it shouldn't be surprising that while my theology and conscious thinking spoke one truth to me, in some subtle ways my feelings had partly been shaped by my culture, which fed me a deceit that went against all that. And when that horrible news of my nephew's death slammed into me one early January morning, the subtle ways my feelings had been shaped by that deceit boiled to the surface.

All of this happened when I was about halfway through writing this book: a book about disciple making as an aspect of Christian discipleship that actually addressed some of the fallacies of the prosperity gospel. As those questions bubbled up, I brought them to God, over and over again over several days and weeks.

A few months before Brad's death, the great writer and spiritual theologian Eugene Peterson passed away. After Peterson's death, I remember

Introduction

watching a short film documentary and interview on YouTube about Peterson's relationship with Bono, the singer-songwriter with the band U2. The piece is titled, simply, "Bono and Eugene Peterson: The Psalms," and much of it is simply a recorded conversation between Bono and Peterson, about the Psalms, which is also a conversation about prayer. Peterson makes the astute and important comment that the Psalms are not about being *nice* to God, but about being *honest* with God. Our prayers and our art should be the same: honest.

In bringing before God those questions about Brad's death—not just questions, but also a certain amount of anger and a sense of loss and even hopelessness—I was at least being honest with God. That honesty helped lead to the realization of how, despite all my protestations about its falseness, I had nonetheless been influenced by one of the most prevalent and harmful American heresies: the false teaching that if we have enough faith in God and in Jesus, or perhaps if we live good lives and go to church and give money to the church (or, more specifically, to the peddlers of this false gospel) that we will be guaranteed wealth, health, and comfort. Though the false message might be vaguely supported by focusing on a few passages from the Bible taken out of context, while ignoring many others, the overall weight of Scripture—including especially the teachings of Jesus and Paul and also the examples of countless saints—strongly refutes it. Though not the main subject of this book, that point kept arising in the central passages that are the main focus. Moreover, those false ideas don't just stay in our heads; they impact how we live: they lead to a pursuit of comfort as a right, and a pursuit of power as a means. Indirectly, the false ideas also result in fear.

Those false ideas get in the way of our being disciples of Christ, and they get in the way of our work of making disciples. Yet there they were, taking root in me, even while I intentionally argued against them. What was not yet complete in me—what will not be complete until Christ returns—was God's transforming work in me: shaping my thoughts and life. Our thoughts are shaped by rational doctrine, but also by experience, and most importantly by the work of the Holy Spirit. How does that happen? Through spiritual renewal. Through transformation. Through discipleship.

This book is about all of that, but especially about the work of disciple making: about not just God's transforming work in our lives, but his working through us in the transformation of other lives. It is, as the title indicates, about disciple making in a culture of power, comfort, and fear.

Introduction

The book is centered on two passages. The first is the book of 2 Timothy, the Apostle Paul's final surviving epistle: a letter written to his close friend, and a sort of sermon on disciple *making*. Outside of the Gospels, 2 Timothy 2:1–6 is my favorite New Testament passage. It has been since 1986 when I spent the summer on a missions project to eastern Europe—to a country closed to the gospel—and spent the whole summer memorizing and in close study of the epistle. In the intervening decades, I have led numerous studies on the book (mostly with college students) and spoken on it several times in churches.

The second passage is a much shorter one: 1 John 2:16. It contains what might be described as a threefold pattern of temptation, or perhaps a threefold categorization of sin. In this passage, John, a disciple of Jesus, writes of the lust of the eyes, the lust of the flesh, and the boastful pride of life—a pattern that can also be seen in the temptation scenes recorded in Genesis 3:1–6 and in Luke 4:1–13.

At first, I saw these two passages—the epistle of 2 Timothy and that passage from 1 John—as exploring two distinct topics, without much close connection. Yet the more I worked on this book, the more I began to see overlapping principles between the topics of disciple making and temptation, especially around themes of obedience, spiritual discipline, and suffering. Just as discipleship has obedience at its core, sin has a *lack* of obedience as its definition. Or we might say that discipleship is centered on faith, and sin is (or is a result of) a lack of faith. Both passages also warn about living in fear and pursuing power. Thus the more I wrote, and the more close relationships I became aware of, the more it seemed like a single cohesive topic rather than two.

1

Disciples as Disciple Makers (and the Importance of Lenses)

Seeing through the Lenses of Cameras and Sunglasses

SEVERAL MONTHS BEFORE I began writing this book, I attended a presentation from a nationally recognized digital forensics expert who specialized in the authenticity and reliability of photographic evidence. He spoke about his work examining digital photographs to determine whether they had been altered. One basic enabling principle of his work is surprising but simple: all camera lenses distort. Not only do lenses distort, but different lenses distort in different unique and predictable ways. They distort shape. They also handle different spectrums of light in different ways in different parts of an image.

Some distortion comes from the environment. Smudges or water drops on a lens distort an image. I have a whole digital photo album of blurred images from a day of steelhead fishing on the Olympic Peninsula, the rainiest region of the continental United States, because I failed to keep my lenses dry that day. If you've ever tried to take a photo through a thick airplane window, or even the curved window of a car, you have likely noticed distortions in the photos. I've been on a small plane in Alaska taking wildlife photos and tried to avoid windshield blur by opening the window and leaning out of the plane, but found that my terror was nearly as great an impediment to good photos as the distortion caused by the window. If the distortion is the result of a poor-quality lens, however, there isn't much you can do. Moreover, some distortion is not merely a result of cheaper lenses; although better lenses distort less than poor quality ones, some distortion is inherent in *all* camera lens—which is one reason the digital forensics techniques are so effective.

Distortion of shape is most obvious in a wide-angle lens, such as a fish-eye. As an avid angler and fishing writer, I use a wide-angle lens and get as close as possible when taking fish photos. This makes the fish appear bigger. It's more than merely having the fish fill the frame, which could be accomplished with a telephoto lens from a great distance; the wide angle expands the background captured in the image, so the fish blocks out a bigger expanse of the distant mountain range. The wider the angle, the more the photo will fatten objects close to the front. At a deeper level, digital forensics takes into account color spectrum and shape and other properties. By looking at the entire image, experts can determine whether the distortions present in each little portion of an image are consistent with the distortion of the image as a whole. Put another way, they can determine whether all of the distortions are consistent with a single lens.

Within a few months of that presentation about digital forensics, two other things happened in my life. First, I purchased a pair of high-end sunglasses (rather than the typical pair found on a pharmacy rack, or the better-quality variety I've purchased at fishing shops). Second—in one of those moments not uncommon for somebody in their mid-fifties, but still coming as unwelcome news—I was told by my eye doctor that I had the start of cataracts as well as deteriorating close-up vision that would require me to purchase my first pair of prescription glasses.

My seemingly extravagant purchase of sunglasses was a pair of Costa lenses with a patented polarizing multi-layer technology. From the moment I donned them, I was enamored. The improvement in my vision was breathtaking. Probably to the annoyance of my family and friends, I began to sound like an advertisement for Costa. But the sunglasses truly were amazing. I saw more sharply than I had ever seen before. Rather than distorting like a camera lens, the multilayer sunglass lenses actually enhanced my vision. They cut out some light from the yellow spectrum—the haze and blur—allowing sharper vision of red, green, and blue, and of contrasts. Cloudscapes took on whole new textures, as did grasses across the treeless Alaskan alpine terrain where I was giving my new lenses their first real trial. The polarization also cuts out glare from reflected light, allowing me to look down *through* the surface of water. Walking along a river with my wife, I'd point out a rainbow trout swimming in the current. Though I could see the fish with great clarity, she'd stare where I was pointing without seeing a thing. I'd take off the lens and realize I couldn't see it anymore, even knowing where to look.

So why I am writing about camera lenses and sunglasses in a book on disciple making? Metaphorically speaking, we all look at the world through lenses. And the important issue is not merely *tint*—whether or not we see through the proverbial rose-colored glasses—but *distortion*. Depending on our cultures, backgrounds, family upbringing, and past experiences, we each see the world differently. And yet those metaphorical camera lenses that offer us our pictures of the world are like our accents in that we are often unaware of them. Most of us are far more cognizant of the accents of others than of our own. Yet, like the optical camera lenses that focus objects onto CMOS chips to store images digitally, the metaphorical cultural lenses we wear also distort. All of them do. Readers of this book who, like me, have grown up in a culture of American consumerism, materialism, and commercialism are inclined to wear a very particular type of distorting lens that values material possessions, power, and individualism (including a stress on individual rights, individual choice, and self-sufficiency). It's not just a matter of taking out a lens cloth and wiping down the lenses (though, metaphorically speaking, that may be a good exercise); the distortion is in the lenses themselves. We need to remove our cultural lenses. And that takes a lot of work. Indeed, we can never wholly remove all of the distorting lenses through which we see the world, nor can we prevent our lenses from continually getting smudged and needing a good wipe.

Unlike the cultural lenses we all wear, however, the word of God does not distort. God's word is true and reliable. It works more like my high quality sunglasses than like a camera lens. It helps us see through the haze, and cuts the glare off shiny objects so we can see them for what they are. God's word reveals the world with greater clarity and sharpness.

Indeed, it does much more than that. When my optometrist gave me the unwelcome news about the start of cataracts, she also emphasized that if I protected my eyes from the sun's damaging rays I might be able to go a couple decades before needing cataract surgery. The fact that my new Costas offered me protection from high-energy visible (HEV) light as well as ultraviolet (UV) rays became more meaningful. Likewise, a deep knowledge of truth is our best protection against deception—against the spiritual blindness that comes from distorting cultural worldviews that pervades even the church. As I wrote in my Introduction, events in my family during the year I was writing this book made me realize the extent to which my own lenses had been distorted by the materialistic, consumerist, capitalistic American culture I have grown up with, so that I saw certain events through the false lens of the prosperity gospel. The truth of Scriptures gave me a foundation to help me recognize the distortions of those lenses.

Being Formed by the Scriptures

A few months before I began writing this book, I stumbled on a quote from author Alan Jacobs:

> The great majority of Christians in America who call themselves evangelical are simply not formed by Christian teaching or the Christian Scriptures. They are, rather, formed by the media they consume—or, more precisely, by the media that consume them. The Bible is just too difficult, and when it's not difficult it is terrifying. So many Christians simply act tribally, and when challenged to offer a Christian justification for their positions typically grope for a Bible verse or two, with no regard for its context or even its explicit meaning.[1]

Jacobs's comment came in response to a politician attempting to use a Bible verse to justify a policy that, to many believing Christians, seemed to have little to do with the teachings of Scripture or with obedience to Christ. Yet the particulars of that moment are in some sense less important than the broader principle. Jacob's critique is both relevant and important to our modern media-saturated time, and should not be dismissed as partisan based on one's stance on the particular issue of that day. The reality is that politicians on both sides of the aisle have routinely quoted (or misquoted) Bible verses with no context and seemingly no understanding of the broader principles of Scriptures. Unfortunately, they often get away with it; many church-goers accept the thin pseudo-biblical justifications, lacking the deeper biblical knowledge to recognize the distortion or misuse. Biblical knowledge within the modern Western Christian church seems to be very shallow.

Probably the easiest response is to point the finger of blame at the teachings of the typical American church on a typical Sunday morning, and

1. Jacobs, "Snakes and Ladders."

Disciples as Disciple Makers (and the Importance of Lenses)

to say that the Bible simply isn't being presented—or at least it is not being taught deeply; in the words of Jacobs, the "difficult" and "challenging" parts are often ignored. There is certainly some truth to that. And yet I have been to numerous churches over the past years, visiting friends and relatives all over the country, and have heard some excellent, deep, challenging teaching from a variety of different pastors in different denominations. In my own church, I am challenged week after week by biblically rooted preaching, and by engagement at a deep level with Scriptures, even the difficult and uncomfortable ones. Could the problem have as much or more to do with a lack of discipleship as with a lack of solid teaching during the Sunday morning worship hour? Or to put it in other terms: that churchgoers are hearing true words, but not being transformed?

Of course, part of the problem is that many American "churchgoers" don't actually "go to church," at least not consistently. Even those who do regularly attend church for a couple hours each week—who are present for twenty to forty minutes of biblically sound preaching, and maybe another forty minutes of exposure to good theology in the form of songs and hymns, Scriptures and liturgy, and perhaps even an hour of adult Sunday school—still go home and spend another 166 hours outside of church. For most of us, that's more than 110 waking hours outside of church for every two hours spent inside of church (which are hopefully also waking hours). In noting this disparity, I am certainly *not* advocating that Christians try to balance that difference by spending fifty-six waking hours in church to match fifty-six waking hours outside of church. This would run counter to both the example and the teachings of Jesus, whose great high priestly prayer (recorded in John 17) was that his followers, though not being *of* this world, would yet remain *in* this world. Indeed, I'm not even advocating an increase to four or five hours a week spent in church. I believe it is *un*healthy (though also comfortable and therefore tempting) for Christians to isolate themselves from the world and live secluded within the safe and comfortable confines of a church. Just being *busy* with church activities is not the answer. Spending time in a building isn't going to transform our lives. In excess, it will effectively cut off our witness.

But consider this also. A 2016 study found that American adults watched more than five hours per day of television.[2] That's startling to me. Terrifying, even. Even if the amount of television-watching was only half as high as claimed—even a third or a fourth of that—it would still be a

2. Koblin, "How Much Do We Love TV?"

DISCIPLE MAKING IN A CULTURE OF POWER, COMFORT, AND FEAR

large volume of television consumption. The good news is that, according to the same survey, the number had been slowly declining—especially the hours spent watching live television. The bad news, however, is that time spent absorbing media content on a tablet or computer is rising dramatically. A 2011 Federal Communications Commission report stated, "The average American spends 70 minutes a day taking in the news, according to the Pew Research Center for the People & the Press," and "that number does not include news read on cell phones, iPads, or other digital devices."[3] A more recent report from Nielsen (July 2018) suggests that adults in the United States now "spend over eleven hours per day listening to, watching, reading, or generally interacting with media."[4] When I say that these later statistics are both startling and in a way horrifying, many Christian readers may assume that I'm primarily critiquing the raunchier content readily available on television and the internet. There is plenty of that, and any amount of time spent consumed by unhealthy content is unhealthy. But I'm primarily referring to the news media, which is primarily just another form of entertainment media, funded by advertising just like your favorite sitcom or drama.

I didn't check reports comparing statistics for churchgoers with non-churchgoers, Christians vs non-Christians, or religious people and nonreligious people. Yet given what I have read about many other cultural phenomena, I'd be surprised if consumption of news media was significantly lower among churchgoers. So, let's consider the Christian who spends a minimum of seventy minutes per day—which sums to more than eight hours a week—with CNN, and less than an hour a week actively engaged in Scripture.

Or perhaps I shouldn't use CNN as my example. Statistics tell us that older white citizens of the United States who consider themselves evangelical Christians overwhelmingly voted for Trump in the elections of November, 2016. It might more relevant (and uncomfortable) to many American Christians, therefore, to consider instead the consumption of Fox News and all its permutations. For the person spending eight hours a week watching Fox and an hour or less a week actively engaged in Scripture, the Bible will not be a lens through which they interpret Fox News, but rather Fox News will become the lens through which they interpret the Scripture. And that, indeed, is a very serious problem, whether it is Fox, or CNN, or any

---

3. Waldman, *The Information Needs of Communities*, 226.
4. Nielsen, "Time Flies."

other source. As Alan Jacobs noted, "They are... formed by the media they consume—or, more precisely, by the media that consume them." The lenses of media will distort.

The Bible must be the lens through which we understand the world. It must be the lens through which we understand Fox or CNN, and not vice versa. And the incarnation, life, death, and especially resurrection of Jesus Christ should be the lens through which we understand Scripture. If that is to be the case, then the Christian church must become a people devoted to a deep, careful, thoughtful understanding of Scripture—not Scripture taken in little bites when convenient, and interpreted through the distorting lens of Fox (or our favorite other media or politician), but Scripture taken at its most difficult and challenging.

And this leads us back to discipleship and to disciple making.

Disciples as Disciple Makers

I am tempted to say we live in the midst of a crisis of discipleship. But I don't like the language of "crisis" any more than I like the language of fear. Fear-mongering is a problem in the church, and not a solution. Crisis language too often leads to language of fear. (In his book *Tell It Slant*, Eugene Peterson writes about the parables Jesus told his disciples while passing through Samaria on his way to his crucifixion. Despite the trials coming very quickly upon Jesus and his followers, Peterson observes, "[I]t is interesting and significant that Jesus doesn't use crisis language. He speaks conversationally, hardly raising his voice."[5] We will return in a later chapter to the important topic of fear.) In any case, discipleship has never been easy. I would say, rather, that we are missing out on the great *opportunities* of discipleship. Consider, for a moment, the final words of Jesus recorded in the Gospel of Matthew, and often referred to as the Great Commission.

> Then Jesus came to them and said, "All authority in heaven and on earth has been given to me. Therefore go and make disciples of all nations, baptizing them in the name of the Father and of the Son and of the Holy Spirit, and teaching them to obey everything I have commanded you. And surely I am with you always, to the very end of the age." (Matthew 28:18-20, NIV)

---

5. Peterson, *Tell It Slant*, 13.

Note first that being a disciple of Christ involves making disciples. The Greek noun *mathétés*, usually translated as "disciple," is used repeatedly through the Gospels to describe Jesus' followers (e.g., John 6:66; 8:31; 13:35; 15:8) and especially his twelve disciples (Matthew 10:1; Luke 22:11). It is also used several times in Acts (Acts 6:1,2,7; 14:20, 22, 28, etc.) to describe the early Christians. *Vine's Expository Dictionary of New Testament Words* describes the meaning of this noun as "a learner . . . indicating thought accompanied by endeavor."[6] That definition is important. It implies that being a disciple involves both how we *think* and how we *act*.

The Great Commission passage above, in Verse 19, uses a verb form of this word: *mathéteuó*. Depending on whether it is used in the active or passive voice, and in a transitive or intransitive form, it can mean to *be* a disciple, to *make* disciples, or to *be made* a disciple. All three of those are important aspects of Christian discipleship. In Matthew 28:19, the verb is used in the active transitive sense, meaning it is a call to make disciples of others. That meaning is also clear from the remainder of the sentence, which goes on to explain that this disciple-*ing*, or disciple making, includes baptizing and teaching.

So Jesus commanded *his* disciples to make *other* disciples. And the rest of that command should make it clear that Jesus' disciples were not the only ones who were supposed to be disciple makers. Jesus also said that those "disciples of all nations" should be taught to obey *all* of the commands Jesus gave to his own disciples, one of which is the very command to make disciples. *Make more disciples and teach them to obey everything I commanded you, including this command to make more disciples.* Thus, to be a disciple of Christ is to be a disciple maker for Christ. Being requires making.

This can be said another way. This important passage is often misunderstood as merely a call to evangelism, as though Jesus had said, "Go into all the world and make converts." The gospel is indeed "good news." That's what the word *gospel* means: it comes from the Old English phrase *gód spel* ("good story"), which was used in the early middle ages to translate the Latin word *evangelium*, which derives from the older Greek *euaggelion* meaning "good message"—a word that appears frequently throughout the New Testament to describe the message or preaching of Christ and about Christ, including for example in Mark 1:1.[7] *Evangelium* shares a root with

---

6. Vine, *Vine's Expository Dictionary of New Testament Words*, 318.
7. In that sense, the term "evangelical Christian" is redundant. The Christian message

Disciples as Disciple Makers (and the Importance of Lenses)

the word for *angel*, which means "messenger." It is also the root of the modern word *evangelism*. The gospel ought to be proclaimed as news, and moreover as good news. We should be excited to proclaim it. However, the Great Commission is much more than that: it is not just a call to make *converts*, but a call to make *disciples*. Central to discipleship is obedience, and part of obeying what is commanded is knowing and understanding those commands. As the definition of "disciple" indicates, to be a disciple involves "thought accompanied by endeavor." Thus, also central to making disciples who obey is "teaching them." That would include, as explicitly stated in this passage, "teaching them ... everything I commanded you."

Discipleship goes far beyond just a set of commands, however. A disciple of Christ is a follower of Christ, is one who knows Christ. To be a disciple of Christ is to allow Christ to transform you. And to be a disciple is also to be a disciple maker, and thus to be involved in that transformation process in the lives of others. The making of disciples therefore also involves more than just making converts; it involves teaching about Christ, which also means teaching about God the Father. This command is for all who claim to follow Christ. To state this as a double negative: those who want to be disciples of Christ are *not* given the option of *not* being involved in the work of disciple making.

It is sad, therefore, to meet Christians who have had bad experiences with discipleship—or with something referred to as "discipleship" that may have had little to do with the biblical model of discipleship. At the worst, this so-called disciple making was abusive or controlling, or just impersonal and merely institutional. Sometimes changing the word and calling it "mentoring" can make it easier. Yet the real solution isn't to throw away the concept or principles of disciple making. It would be better to reclaim both the word and the concept. As noted above, being and making disciples is central to the life of the Christian. Maybe part of the problem is that some Christians often try to make disciples for themselves rather than for Christ. But that should not be the goal. I am called to make disciples of Christ, and not disciples of Matthew Dickerson, or of my pastor, or of some charismatic television personality or megachurch leader. Only of Christ.

---

is the gospel, the good news, the *evangelium*. Being a Christian involves believing that gospel. One cannot be a Christian apart from the *evangelium*. Unfortunately, the term *evangelical* has been absconded to take on numerous political connotations that sometimes have little or nothing to do with the gospel. Rather than give up on a term that is central to Christianity, I believe it is better to use the term, but only with its biblical meaning. A similar comment could be made about the word *discipleship*.

Likewise, I cannot do the transforming work myself—not even in my own life and certainly not in somebody else's. The transforming work can only be done by God, by the Holy Spirit's work in our lives. (We will return to this, especially in the chapters 6 and 7.)

The Apostle Paul understood this. The final bit of writing we have remaining from Paul—perhaps the last letter he wrote or dictated—is his second letter to his friend Timothy, a fellow disciple of Christ and one whom Paul helped make into a disciple. Second Timothy reads almost like a sermon on Matthew 28:18–20, which would make sense if it is indeed Paul's final guide to disciple making written to the disciple he was closest to. Consider for a moment just one observation from 2 Timothy 2:2, which states (in the NIV translation), "And the things you have heard me say in the presence of many witnesses entrust to reliable people who will also be qualified to teach others." Note that this one verse mentions four generations[8] of disciples of Christ. Paul (the "me" of this verse) is the first generation listed here, and Timothy (the "you" in this passage) is the second; Paul has passed the gospel on to Timothy, his spiritual child. But it doesn't end with Timothy, the second generation, as we might expect in this personal letter; it continues for two more generations. Timothy is told to pass the gospel on to "reliable people" (the third generation), and they in turn are expected to "teach others" (the fourth generation.) Paul seems to be telling Timothy, *You have not yet finished passing on the gospel and the gospel life—your work as a maker of disciples isn't done—until those you have passed the gospel on to are themselves passing it on to others.* Or perhaps Paul is saying about himself, *My disciple-making work with Timothy is not complete until Timothy is making disciples of others, and Timothy's disciples are also making disciples.* This is precisely the message Jesus was giving to his own disciples: Jesus' disciples were to be making disciples, and passing on to them the same instruction to be disciple makers.

The first part of this book (following this introductory chapter) is a look at 2 Timothy, and especially 2 Timothy 2:2. Paul provides three important principles of disciple making. These principles will lead to discipleship continuing far beyond the second generation:

---

8. I use the term *generations* here in keeping with Paul's own metaphor of "parent-child" that he uses frequently to refer to his relationship with Timothy, simply extending that relationship to those who might later be considered the spiritual children of Timothy. We will explore this relational aspect of discipleship more in chapter 3.

Disciples as Disciple Makers (and the Importance of Lenses)

1. Christian disciple making is rooted in the word of God.
2. Christian disciple making is relational.
3. Christian disciple making takes place in the context of Christian fellowship and the Christian church.

Chapters 2, 3, and 4 explore these three principles. Chapter 5 looks at three metaphors Paul uses in 2 Timothy 2:3–6 to help illuminate these principles (for Timothy and for us). Chapters 6 and 7 then explore obedience and transformation, as well as sin and temptation, in the context of discipleship and disciple making. The final chapter then seeks to answer the question, "What might this look like in a church today?"

I don't claim to be writing anything new here. If I thought I had written something really new, I would be nervous it was wrong. In trying to be true to the teachings of Jesus, and of the Spirit-inspired Scriptures coming to us through authors like Paul, I want to continually point back to the Bible, and therefore to what countless disciples of Christ have taught or written about in the past. In order to help us all replace the distorting lens of our culture with the clarifying lens of God's word, I need to let the Bible be my own lens for writing about disciple making. As I noted earlier, I've been fortunate (and blessed) to have been nurtured in my life by many great mentors, teachers, and models (beginning with my own parents), who have influenced me through their writing or teaching. Many writers have shaped not only my biblical theology, but also my moral imagination—I think especially of J. R. R. Tolkien and C. S. Lewis—and my theological imagination.

"Theological imagination?" you ask. That sounds dangerous. One can't simply imagine a theology. That is to say, lots of people attempt to imagine a theology that is comfortable and convenient. It is quite popular in our modern relativistic culture to just make up a set of beliefs: "I like to think of God as <fill-in-the-blank>." But I'm not interested in any made-up theology. I am interested in knowing what is true, and living that out. And our imaginations are vitally important in that task. Consider first how often Paul speaks in metaphor. For example, beginning in 2 Timothy 2:3, he provides three metaphors for what the life of discipleship is like: a soldier, an athlete, and a farmer. Thus Paul engages Timothy's imagination.

Jesus does the same. He speaks in metaphor and story even more often than Paul. One reason for this may be that a true understanding of God transcends our rational ability to comprehend. It transcends the effort to reduce theology to a set of propositions, which is yet another form of idolatry. Propositions are important, certainly. But alone they are insufficient. I affirm that Jesus was simultaneously fully human and fully divine. That affirmation is important. It is central to every Christian creed. Yet I don't come close to fully grasping what it means, and the extent to which I do grasp it comes as much from imaginatively engaging with the story of the Gospels, and the metaphors of Christ, as with any statement about the Gospels. In his book *The Jesus Way*, Eugene Peterson writes:

> The simple fact is that life is mostly invisible, inaudible, untouchable. Life may be ultimately inaccessible to our five senses, but without the evidence supplied by our five senses it would for the most part elude us. It turns out that the quickest and most available access to the invisible by means of language is through metaphor, a word that names the visible (or audible, or touchable). A metaphor is a word that carries us across the abyss separating the invisible from the visible. The contradiction involved in what the word denotes and what it connotes sets up a tension in our minds, and we are stimulated to an act of imagination in which we become participants in what is being spoken. Metaphor is our lexical witness to transcendence—to the more, the beyond, the within—to all that cannot be accounted for by our microscopes and telescopes, by our algebra and geometry, by pulse rate and blood pressure, by weights and measures . . . a witness to all the operations of the Trinity.[9]

No wonder then, given the importance of our imagination and thus also of metaphor, that—as Peterson goes on to say—"The writers of Scripture are all masters of metaphor, language as a witness to the interconnectedness of all things visible and invisible."[10]

Yet another way that imagination is important is in shaping our lives. "How rare," author Dick Keyes noted in his book *Beyond Identity*, "are writers like C. S. Lewis whose genius as a writer of fiction lay in his ability to make moral goodness attractive and heroic."[11] That idea is so important that Keyes went on to write another book entirely on heroism. In *From Homer to Harry Potter: a Handbook of Myth and Fantasy*, a book I co-wrote with my friend David O'Hara about imaginative literature, we also explore

---

9. Peterson, *The Jesus Way*, 25.
10. Peterson, *The Jesus Way*, 25.
11. Keyes, *Beyond Identity*, 21.

Disciples as Disciple Makers (and the Importance of Lenses)

how our actions are often far more inspired by our heroes (whom we seek to imitate, whether consciously or not) than by abstract moral principles.

This is another reason why disciple making is so important, and a point I explore in chapter 4: the making of disciples is not merely a matter of passing on teaching, doctrine, or theology, but of passing on a life, of modeling Christ-likeness. It is the work of transformation: of opening ourselves up to God's transforming work in our lives, and to being a part of his transforming work in the lives of others. Thus equally important to the knowledge many have passed on to me through books are the examples they have been for me, inspiring me want to live the life of a disciple. I hope this book is helpful to those who also want to live that life.

2

Disciple Making and the Word of God

> *And the things you have heard me say* in the presence of many witnesses entrust to reliable people who will also be qualified to teach others.
>
> —2 Timothy 2:2, NIV, emphasis added

My wife and I have raised three sons. They have all grown into wonderful adult men. Recognizing that child-raising is not something we have done alone, but a task for which we were dependent on the Holy Spirit and which the entire church has been involved in—our local congregation as well as the church universal—we are often thankful for other Christian mentors and leaders who invested in the lives of our sons. We think of youth group and Young Life leaders, pastors, staff with campus Christian ministries, and perhaps most often just other caring adults in our church and various churches they have been a part of. It has been a delight watching that process over the years, though not without challenges.

One of the things my sons inherited from me is selective hearing, though they each practiced it in their own unique ways. One son was very good at nodding his head when we spoke and even giving verbal assent without actually *hearing* (in any meaningful sense) a single word we said. His thoughts were off somewhere in his own world, or on whatever book or task or toy he happened to have in front of him. We would be going away for

Disciple Making and the Word of God

an evening and would make it very clear there was just one thing he needed to do (or not do), only to return and find that he had neglected to do that one thing we asked of him (or done the one thing we asked him not to do). And he would claim, with seeming sincerity, that we'd never told him that. What he meant, of course—and could probably say with honesty—is that he'd never *heard* us say that.

So my wife and I eventually learned our parenting lesson. Before giving him any instructions, we would force him to put down whatever he was doing, stand before us, and look into our eyes as we spoke (a process akin to pulling teeth). We then required him to repeat back to us what we had just told him (sometimes three or four times). My wife and I would then verify with each other, in front of him, that the conversation had taken place. We were all witnesses. That repetition still didn't guarantee that our son would remember what we'd told him more than five minutes after we left, but it helped some. There were things he had heard from *us*, and we all knew what those things were.

The Things You Have Heard Me Say: The Standard of Sound Teaching

"And the things you have heard me say in the presence of many witnesses entrust to reliable people who will also be qualified to teach others." Paul wrote those words to Timothy, his friend, fellow disciple, and fellow disciple maker. They come to us in Paul's letter, written from prison months or perhaps even weeks or days before his death as he awaited his imminent execution ordered by Emperor Nero. Timothy was one of the disciples Paul helped to make as he carried out the great disciple-making commission—not a disciple of himself, but a disciple of Christ. At the time Paul wrote this letter, Timothy was a pastor of the church at Ephesus where Paul had helped establish him[1] sometime between Paul's first imprisonment in Rome (recorded at the end of Acts) and the writing of 1 Timothy. This was followed by Paul's second and more brutal imprisonment when he wrote the letter we know as 2 Timothy.

As a pastor in Ephesus, Timothy himself was also involved in disciple making as he had witnessed Paul do for many years. Paul's letter was a

---

1. See, for example, 1 Timothy 1:3-4. See also the Introduction to John Stott's *The Message of 2 Timothy* for more background on the context of the letter as well as a defense of its authenticity.

guide for Timothy in this work. The command in 2:2 has always seemed to me the central charge of the letter: the primary message that the earlier part of the letter introduces and the remainder of the letter elaborates upon. Even more specifically, the opening phrase of this verse is a central topic of 2 Timothy (and of this book): "*And the things you have heard me say.*"

But what, exactly, *did* Timothy hear Paul say? What are those "things" Paul is referring to? The word translated as "things" in the NIV is often translated as "which," and must be understood in the context of the following phrase "from me" or "beside me." The verb "say" doesn't appear at all in the original Greek and is only implied. So the opening of this sentence might be translated, "And *that which* you have heard *from me*," or perhaps, less awkwardly, "And what you have heard from me." The emphasis, therefore, is on the words "from me"; it is what gives context to "the things." Reading those words, Timothy should be thinking of what he heard *from Paul*.

And what is that? The answer to that question runs throughout the entire epistle. Paul comes back to it repeatedly, and it leads to the main point of this chapter. *Christian disciple making is rooted in the word of God*; it must be centered on Scripture, on the gospel: on Christ and the teachings of Christ.

The centrality of the word of God in Christian disciple making should be an obvious point, and yet I think all who have sought to follow Christ as disciples and disciple makers can probably acknowledge that it is easy to get sidetracked. So let's consider this more deeply.

Second Timothy 2:2 is not the first time in this letter Paul uses this phrase, *ekousas par emou* in the Greek. Earlier on, in the paragraph following his personal introduction, Paul also writes to Timothy of "What you heard from me." The original Greek of 1:13 is close to 2:2. It might also be translated as "the words [sayings] which you heard from me." Here is the passage in full:

> 8 So do not be ashamed of the testimony about our Lord or of me his prisoner. Rather, join with me in suffering for the gospel, by the power of God. 9 He has saved us and called us to a holy life—not because of anything we have done but because of his own purpose and grace. This grace was given us in Christ Jesus before the beginning of time, 10 but it has now been revealed through the appearing of our Savior, Christ Jesus, who has destroyed death and has brought life and immortality to light through the gospel. 11 And of this gospel I was appointed a herald and an apostle and

> a teacher. 12 That is why I am suffering as I am. Yet this is no cause for shame, because I know whom I have believed, and am convinced that he is able to guard what I have entrusted to him until that day.
>
> 13 What you heard from me, keep as the pattern of sound teaching, with faith and love in Christ Jesus. 14 Guard the good deposit that was entrusted to you—guard it with the help of the Holy Spirit who lives in us. (2 Timothy 1:8–14, NIV)

We asked what Timothy heard from Paul. What is discipleship built upon? Another way to phrase that question would be to ask, "What is Paul's testimony?" Paul provides an answer with a short summary reminder of his testimony for which he was willing to suffer as a prisoner. One important observations comes from 1:8. Paul associates his own testimony with the testimony about his Lord, Jesus Christ. This must always be the case for a disciple and disciple maker of Christ: our testimony must be a testimony of and about Jesus. When Paul writes about "the things you have heard from me," he is speaking of the testimony about his Lord Jesus.

A second observation from verse 8 clarifies that further: first and foremost, Paul's testimony is the gospel itself: the good news of Jesus Christ and salvation by grace. (Note that both of these words, *gospel* and *grace,* are used twice in this passage, following two earlier references to *gospel* in the introduction to this letter.)

Paul goes on, then, to give a wonderful pithy summary of that gospel, which is his testimony. His summary has several points, including:

1. It is a gospel of salvation. (God has saved us.)
2. Jesus is the means of that salvation. (It is a gospel of grace and not salvation by works.)
3. It is a gospel of hope. (Jesus destroyed death and brought about eternal life.)
4. The gospel has been at work for all eternity.
5. It is a gospel that calls us to a holy life.

Each of those points are well worth dwelling on, repeatedly, earnestly, intentionally. This gospel summary is thus the context—the testimony of Paul—when Paul refers to the *words* (1:13) or *things* (2:2) that Timothy has heard *from him*. This gospel, and the testimony of this gospel from Paul and later Timothy, is central to disciple making.

That is also why it is central to this letter. John Stott, in his work *The Message of 2 Timothy*, writes that we can "summarize the message of the letter in terms of a four-fold charge" with all four parts centering on the gospel. Stott's summary is as follows:

Chapter 1: The charge to guard the gospel.

Chapter 2: The charge to suffer for the gospel.

Chapter 3: The charge to continue in the gospel.

Chapter 4: The charge to proclaim the gospel.[2]

If we understand "continue in the gospel" as living a life of obedience, Stott's fourfold summary of 2 Timothy could be a summary of Christian discipleship itself. Consider how Paul continues the letter after his summary. His next sentence is a command: *keep this gospel you have heard from me as the pattern or standard of sound teaching*. The disciple of Christ has a duty to suffer for gospel, and also a duty to guard it. Disciple making is the central strategy for guarding the gospel; we guard it—that is, keep it from being lost or distorted—by passing it on in its true form.

The Revised Standard Version (RSV) translates the command in verse 14: "Guard the truth that has been entrusted to you by the Holy Spirit who dwells within us." Stott writes the following about "Paul's double exhortation" in verses 13 to 14: "Here Paul refers to the gospel, the apostolic faith, by two expressions. It is both a pattern of sound words (13) and a precious deposit (14)." Stott goes on to point out, "For the gospel is a treasure—a good, noble and precious treasure—deposited for safe keeping within the church. Christ had entrusted it to Paul, and Paul now entrusts it to Timothy."[3] Again, this is at the core of disciple making. It is a passing on and entrusting of the good deposit of God's word, the gospel message of Jesus.

I wrote near the start of this chapter that disciple making must be rooted in the word of God. The reason for this is that the very purpose of disciple making can be said to *be* the word of God. The gospel is both the *means* and the *end* of disciple making.

---

2. Stott, *The Message of 2 Timothy*, 21.
3. Stott, *The Message of 2 Timothy*, 43–44.

Disciple Making and the Word of God

Disciples and Disciple Makers as Craftspersons

Christian disciple making is rooted in the word of God. That is the first of the three major principles. I earlier claimed that this message runs throughout 2 Timothy, and not just verse 2:2. We have already seen the centrality of the gospel in Second Timothy 1. We need look no further than 2 Timothy 2:8–10 to see it again.

> 8 Remember Jesus Christ, raised from the dead, descended from David. This is my gospel, 9 for which I am suffering even to the point of being chained like a criminal. But God's word is not chained. 10 Therefore I endure everything for the sake of the elect, that they too may obtain the salvation that is in Christ Jesus, with eternal glory. (2 Timothy 2:8–10, NIV)

Again, we see Paul mentioning his own suffering, and the importance of being willing to suffer and endure for the gospel. This follows yet another reminder or summary of a central aspect of the gospel, even more concise than the summary in the previous chapter. Here Paul reminds Timothy of the core tenet of the incarnation: Jesus Christ is both fully human ("descended from David") and also divine (confirmed by the fact that he was "raised from the dead"). He then points out that salvation and eternal life—not just eternal life, but eternal *glory*—comes through Jesus Christ. *Remember this*, he tells Timothy. *Focus on it. Don't get distracted. This is worth enduring everything for.* All the work of disciple making is meaningless if it loses sight of the gospel message. Indeed, it is not Christian disciple making at all.

After this summary—that is, with this summary as a reminder and a context—Paul then issues a command to Timothy illuminated by a metaphor that is central to this the chapter.

> 14 Keep reminding God's people of these things. Warn them before God against quarreling about words; it is of no value, and only ruins those who listen. 15 Do your best to present yourself to God as one approved, a worker who does not need to be ashamed and who correctly handles the word of truth. (2 Timothy 2:14–15, NIV)

What things is Timothy supposed to remind God's people of? The start of verse 14 is a reference back to the previous part of the letter. "These things" are the same things Paul just reminded Timothy of: the message of the gospel of salvation. But in verse 15, Paul uses a new expression: *logon tes aletheias*, "the word of truth." *Logon* is the same word Paul used back in 1:13, meaning "words" or "sayings." So in one way this just continues the same message: the things, words, or sayings Timothy heard from Paul (which is Paul's testimony, which is the testimony of the Lord) is what Timothy needs to handle correctly. Here, however, it has an added emphasis: these are words *of truth*. The gospel is not merely a nice story, but a true story.

J. R. R. Tolkien, in his essay "On Fairy-Stories," said it well using a term he coined himself: *eucatastrophe*. Tolkien's new word draws on the same *eu-* prefix as the word *euaggelion*, *"good message"*; a *eucatastrophe* is a "good catastrophe," or more accurately in Tolkien's definition a "sudden joyous 'turn,'" or "sudden and miraculous grace" in a story, a "fleeting glimpse of Joy, Joy beyond the walls of the world, poignant as grief."[4] Here is what Tolkien writes about the gospel.

> But this [gospel] story has entered History and the primary world; the desire and aspiration of sub-creation has been raised to the fulfillment of Creation. The Birth of Christ is the eucatastrophe of Man's history. The Resurrection is the eucatastrophe of the story of the Incarnation. This story begins and ends in joy. It has preeminently the "inner consistency of reality." There is no tale ever told that men would rather find was true, and none which so many skeptical men have accepted as true on its own merits . . . This story is supreme; and it is true.[5]

The gospel is "good news" both because it tells of a wonderful and joyous grace, but also good because it is true. And because it is true, it is all the more important to handle it correctly and pass it on uncorrupted. The Bible must be the lens through which we see the world. And Christians, furthermore, understand the gospel and especially the resurrection to be the lens that gives the most clear understanding of the Bible as a whole. Every other lens will distort.

This is at the core of Paul's raising up of Timothy as a disciple *of* Christ, and it is the core of Timothy's work of disciple making *for* Christ: raising up the folk of his Ephesian church as disciples. And, of course, it must be at the core of our own work as disciple makers. Thus Paul elaborates on this important idea in imaginative terms with the metaphor of an approved worker. What is the "approved worker"? The idea of a craftsperson is one good modern metaphor that captures some of this essence of a "worker."

---

4. Tolkien, "On Fairy-Stories," 153.
5. Tolkien, "On Fairy-Stories," 156–57.

Disciple Making and the Word of God

We are to have the same attitude toward God's word, the word of truth, as a craftsperson has toward her craft. Think of a woodworker, carpenter, or builder. She needs to have intimate knowledge of different types of woods and the properties of each, such as how the grains are aligned, how hard or soft the wood is, how or where it is likely to split or warp, what each type of wood is good for. She must also have a knowledge of the many different tools needed for working that wood, and how each is to be held and used. In short, the skilled woodworker strives for ever-increasing knowledge of the material she works with while continually working to master the tools for doing that work.

Likewise, we need to approach the word of God as craftspeople, seeking to know it intimately and to know also the tools for studying it, or handling it correctly. Different types of wood must be handled in different ways and worked with different tools. So, too, must the disciple of Christ approach different types of Scripture in different ways. For example, there is a difference between how we ought to approach poetry (such as we find in the Psalms) and how we approach the theological teaching of a Pauline epistle; there ought to be a difference between how we approach those epistles (which are frequently prescriptive) and how we approach the narratives in the book of Acts (which are primarily descriptive.) The Chroniclers of the history of Israel and Judah were writing in a different literary mode than the prophets.

I have met many Christians who, in sincere desire to be faithful to Scripture, insist that *all* Scripture must be understood only in a literal sense—all approached in the same way, regardless of purpose, author, mode of literature, or cultural background. Although the intent might be to honor the Bible and give it high worth, in practice it does rather than opposite: it devalues Scripture and fails to treat it as the craftsperson of Paul's metaphor ought to treat it. At the end of the previous chapter, I quoted Eugene Peterson writing about metaphor in his book *The Jesus Way*. In that same passage, Peterson goes on to write: "The writers of Scripture are all masters of metaphor, language as a witness to the interconnectedness of all things visible and invisible. A metaphor takes a word that is commonly used to refer to a thing or action that we experience by means of our five senses and then uses it to refer to something that is beyond the reach of our immediate senses."[6] Examples abound, including in Jesus' own speech. In his teaching recorded in John 6, Jesus repeats the claim, "I am

---

6. Peterson, *The Jesus Way*, 25.

the bread of life." We know that Jesus was not made out of grain. His words are intended to be understood as metaphor, not as a literal or scientific description of his substance. When approached as metaphor they speak richly and powerfully. Likewise, though he said "I am the vine," we are not therefore supposed to think he is a plant; though he said "I am the sheep gate," we shouldn't conclude that he was made of wood and rocks. There are passages of Scripture that certainly must be understood literally, such as proclamations of the resurrection of Jesus—without which Christianity is a meaningless futile religion as Paul makes clear in 1 Corinthians 15. There are also passages that are clearly metaphorical, such as some of the "I am" statements of Jesus referenced above. And there are some more challenging passages which may take some hard work to understand whether they ought to be understood literally or metaphorically. When Jesus said "And if your right hand causes you to stumble, cut it off and throw it away" (Matthew 5:30, NIV), was he speaking literally or metaphorically? What would it even mean for our hand to cause us to stumble? Does a hand make decisions? That is precisely why we must approach Scripture like careful and knowledgeable craftspeople as Paul's metaphor suggests. (Even Paul's use of "workman" to refer to our approach to Scripture is a metaphor.) Just as the knowledge and skills of an expert woodworker don't come overnight, but through time, practice, love, labor, and mentorship under another experienced woodworker, so too does the ability to approach the more difficult passages of Scripture.

Note in particular the goal of the workmanlike approach to Scripture. John Stott points out that the Greek *orthotomounta*, translated by the NIV as "correctly handle" has the connotation of making a straight cut. The ability to cut a straight line would indeed be important to a craftsperson, but Stott suggests the metaphor is closer to that of an engineer cutting a straight road across the countryside, or a farmer ploughing a straight furrow across the field.[7] All three are apt metaphors. We should have the same care for God's word as the farmer has for the furrow, the carpenter for cutting wood, or the engineer for the making of roads. Christian disciple making should encourage engagement with the Scriptures. It should reflect on Scriptures. The disciple *of* Christ working as a disciple maker *for* Christ should model this engagement and reflection.

This careful workmanlike attitude of the approved engineer, farmer, or craftsperson, of course, precludes the abuse of Scripture: the misquoting

---

7. Stott, *The Message of 2 Timothy*, 67.

of passages or taking them out of context in order to justify ourselves (whether our actions are biblically justifiable or not). Not surprisingly, therefore, discipleship is an important part of the "solution" to the problem mentioned in opening chapter in the quote from Alan Jacobs. The practice of discipleship is the practice (to borrow from Jacobs's words) of being "formed by Christian teaching or the Christian Scriptures," and disciple making involves helping others to be formed in the same way. Such practice helps protect us and others from merely acting tribally: from both making or being fooled (in the words of Jacobs) by a shallow groping "for a Bible verse or two, with no regard for its context or even its explicit meaning" in order to justify a position. It is an intentional practice of removing the distorting lenses of our media-saturated and consumerist-driven culture to see instead through the clarifying lens of the Scriptures.

This may also be why Paul issues multiple warnings to Timothy about bad teaching or false doctrine, for example in 2 Timothy 2:14–18, and again in 3:6–9, and again in 3:13, and yet again in 4:3–4. False teaching is poisonous. False teaching leads to false concepts of God. Uli Chi, writing a devotional essay on Matthew 25:24–25 and the parable of the Talents, comments on how false concepts of God can lead to destructive life choices—like burying our talents in the ground because we have a false view of God as vindictive and unjust. The antidote to the poison of these false concepts is true understanding of God, which comes from being biblically rooted. "One of the challenging parts of the Christian journey is to undo our misconceptions of God. However we accumulate such conceptions, it's important that we replace them with a biblically rooted vision of what God is like."[8]

To phrase this in the terms of disciple making, we need to remember that the goal of discipleship is to be like Christ. We ought to be imitators of Christ. And to imitate Christ we must know him and have a true understanding of him. If we have a false concept of God—one shaped by culture, or by Fox or CNN news media, or by American consumerism and materialism—we therefore also have a false understanding of Christ who is God incarnate, and thus we will be imitating a false concept and not the true Christ; we then become disciples of an idol rather than disciples of Christ. Of course knowing God—both Christ the Son and God the Father—is far more than mere intellectual knowledge. It is more than simply affirming a set of doctrines, or an abstract theology, no matter how true

---

8. Chi, "What Is God Like."

those doctrines are. Yet the theology is still important. True understanding comes from personal relationship, and from the work of the Holy Spirit, and from being biblically rooted.

Before continuing, however, it is worth noting that while good teaching and sound understanding is important, the making of disciples does not require one to have a full or perfect knowledge or understanding of Scripture. Indeed, that would be impossible. We approach disciple making as co-learners. We are not making disciples of or for ourselves, but of and for Christ. And before Christ we are all co-learners. (We will return to this notion in the next chapter.) Indeed, the proper attitude of humility toward Scripture might best be exhibited by a willingness to confess our lack of knowledge.

Training in Righteousness

So far in speaking of the importance of Scripture, I have focused on the specific message of the gospel of Jesus and salvation by grace: the good news of the birth, death, and resurrection of Jesus, God incarnate, the Word made flesh. In the first two chapters of his letter, Paul mentions *gospel* five times, and also refers to the "word of truth" and the "testimony about our Lord." Each time he does so, he refers to the story of the incarnation. As J. R. R. Tolkien noted, the story of Jesus is the eucatastrophe of all history, and the resurrection is the eucatastrophe of the story of Jesus. So Paul is right in focusing on that. This gospel story is the central story of Christianity, and is part of what for modern Christians is the Bible, the word of God, holy Scriptures.

There is a strong argument, however, that the gospel is only fully understood in the context of the entirety of Scripture, and thus even in speaking of the importance of the gospel (or the gospels) narrowly understood as the story of Christ, the importance of the entire Bible is implied. Paul's writing about the gospel, for example, doesn't allow his readers to view the rest of the Bible as unimportant. As he continues this letter, he writes about "Holy Scriptures" in their entirety—a phrase that for a Jew like Paul educated to be a religious leader would encompass all Hebrew Scriptures including the Law and the Prophets. Consider what Paul writes in 3:14–17—perhaps the most oft-quoted passage from this epistle—about the importance of Holy Scriptures in Timothy's work as disciple and disciple maker:

Disciple Making and the Word of God

> 14 But as for you, continue in what you have learned and have become convinced of, because you know those from whom you learned it, 15 and how from infancy you have known the Holy Scriptures, which are able to make you wise for salvation through faith in Christ Jesus. 16 All Scripture is God-breathed and is useful for teaching, rebuking, correcting and training in righteousness, 17 so that the servant of God may be thoroughly equipped for every good work. (2 Timothy 2:14–17, NIV)

The fact that Paul references Scriptures that Timothy has known from his infancy makes it clear he is addressing not merely the story of Jesus, but the accepted canon of Jewish Scripture. Paul lets Timothy know that all of it is important; it is all part of the word of truth. What is also clear from the emphasis on the gospel of Jesus Christ is that the gospel is a central aspect of that word of truth. To phrase this in the metaphor with which I began this book: *the Bible is the clarifying lens through which we should see the world; the story of the incarnation—the life of Jesus, the Word made flesh—is the lens through which we should see and understand the whole of Scripture; and the resurrection is the lens through which we should see and understand the gospel.*

Since these verses are well-known, and oft-quoted, I won't write too much more about this passage except to make a few observations central to the topic of disciple making. The first and most important is to keep in mind the purpose or end goal that Paul gives here: that the follower or servant of Christ—the one seeking to learn and obey what Christ has taught—become equipped for the good work God calls us to. That is a wonderful succinct statement of the work of disciple making. It also gets at why disciple making is a challenge. I think of the 1985 film *Silverado*, my favorite Western and one of my all-time favorite movies. The character Hannah (played by Rosanna Arquette) says to Paden (Kevin Cline): "I want to build something. Make things grow. That takes hard work. A lifetime of it. That's not why a man comes to a pretty woman. After a while I won't be so pretty. But this land will be."[9] Hannah's vision is a compelling and worthwhile one: caring for land, making things grow, building something good. The power of that vision is enhanced for viewers by a camera panning over a beautiful landscape. But as she points out, it's a vision that requires work, and it's certainly not the reason that Paden is coming to a pretty woman at that moment in the film.

9. *Silverado*.

In a similar way, people too often come to Christ thinking it is a means to some sort of worldly prosperity, or at least a means toward personal fulfillment. They come thinking they can take Christ as savior without taking him as Lord. They come for eternal life, but not obedience. In their 2005 book *Soul Searching*, Christian Smith and Melinda Lundquist Denton coined a term to describe this false view of Christianity: they called it *moralistic therapeutic deism*.[10] The term *deism* implies a God who isn't really involved in our lives (or in the world)—except perhaps when we are in desperate need and call out for help; *therapeutic* suggests a religion that is about making us feel good, as though it were merely a form of therapy; and *moralistic* gives a nod to the fact that people want to be basically nice—and more importantly they want people around them to be nice—though they don't really want to be transformed through anything as radical as obedience and commitment. We come looking for a god to do those things for us in the same way that Paden has come to Hannah.

The Great Commission, by contrast, is a commission to make disciples of Christ who follow and obey him. Like Hannah's vision for the land, there is a wonderful and joyous process of making and growing and building something good, and there is a beautiful land to dwell in, but it is also a vision for a lifetime of work—joyous and meaningful work to be sure, but work. Discipleship rooted in Scripture equips us for that good work.

Let me return one more time to my new Costa sunglasses. One other feature of the model I chose also related to my age. Although at the time of this writing, my distance vision was still better than 20-20, for half a decade I'd been struggling to focus on objects closer than two and a half feet from my face. My wife was the first to notice that I often squinted when reading, especially if the print was small, or the lights dim, or I was tired. By the time I reached my mid-fifties, I owned several pairs of non-prescription reading glasses that I kept in various places: my desk at work, the bedside table, my office at home, my briefcase. Reading, however, wasn't the biggest issue. More problematic was tying on flies when fishing. Several evening fishing excursions had been either cut short because I couldn't see to tie on a new fly, or had proven unfruitful when I continued using a fly that wasn't working because I couldn't see well enough to replace it. Thus, for my new Costa lenses I selected a "reader" model: sunglasses with built-in magnifiers in the bottoms of the lenses. They not only helped me see distant cloudscapes, tundra grasses, and fish with greater clarity, but also magnified objects that

---

10. Smith and Denton, *Soul Searching*.

were close up and small but very important. The ability to thread fine fishing line through the tiny eye of a fly is vital to fishing.

It is easy to lose sight of what's important. This is especially true if we spend a lot of time saturated by the consumerism and materialism of media culture—even news media culture—or if we have replaced Christianity with moralistic therapeutic deism. Disciple making rooted in Scriptures, in the gospel, in the resurrection, helps us see with more clarity and to see what is really important: details which may appear small or insignificant, but are in fact *crucial*.

On Faithfulness and Exhortation

I was fortunate to grow up in a home with loving parents. The parent-child metaphor for a disciple-making relationship (which we explore in the next chapter) communicates to me something very encouraging, nurturing, and supportive. I have a vivid memory of my father standing out on a cold ski hill in winter watching me race slalom in high school. He stood in the snow shivering for an hour and a half so that he would be there to cheer me at the bottom after the thirty-five-second window that was my brief turn to ski down through the gates. I don't know how many hours my mother spent listening to her sons play music in middle school or high school concerts, but I do know that she was always among the first to read any of my books as soon as they were published, and thus even in my adult years she continued to be the encouraging parent.

Parents, however—at least those who love their children—also want their children to grow and mature. No loving parent really wants a teenager still acting like an eight-year-old, or a thirty-year-old acting like a teenager. Most parents hope one day to successfully launch their children into adulthood. Although there is no narrow rigid formula for disciple making, there are important elements of successful Christ-centered disciple making. One aspect is a desire for spiritual growth. Disciple making is rooted in the word of God, and that word is profitable for exhortation. Those invested in disciple making should be intentional in encouraging growth of the disciple. That should involve elements of challenge, which may be uncomfortable. Indeed, it almost certainly *will* be uncomfortable at times; it *ought* to be, or else growth probably isn't occurring. Just as our children sometimes need to be nudged out of the safety of the nest and into the world, encouraged to seek a job, or work harder at studies, or eat a more healthy diet, so too the disciple-making relationship should involve spiritual growth.

When I was a graduate student, I was involved in a large Christian ministry on campus with several full-time staff members. I remember one fall a staff member asking me if I was considering joining several other staff and students from the region on a summer missions trip to eastern Europe. She didn't put any pressure on me, or try to manipulate me with guilt. But the question was out there. *Am I considering it? Would I consider it?*

I also remember my first definitive response to this challenge. *No. I am not considering it.* I didn't explain my reasoning, but I certainly had my reasons. The main one popped into my head the instant the question was asked: I was in my twenties and didn't own a car, and therefore my social life as well as my outdoor recreation activities were (in my opinion) significantly hindered; for the first time in my life I was getting paid to be a student, and not paying tuition; since I didn't need summer salary for tuition, I could be free to use my summer salary to buy a car; but only if I actually had a summer salary, which I wouldn't have if I went on a summer missions project. What I didn't want to think about, because it made me feel uncomfortable, was that not having to pay tuition for graduate school also meant I was free (for the first time in five years) to choose not to have a summer job and to do something else instead—like going on a missions project. And so that little challenge from a staff member in the campus ministry just to consider a summer ministry opportunity proved the impetus that ultimately led me to a lot of prayer, an uncomfortable reconsideration of my motives, and ultimately to going on the project, which proved one of the more significant periods of my life in terms of my own growth as a disciple.

This sort of challenge or exhortation doesn't need to be big and grand. One of the most important things we can do in disciple making is encourage others to spend time daily in prayer and in reading and studying of Scripture. Without that, there will be little or no growth. As relationships progress, and the disciple grows in faith, a next appropriate challenge or place for growth might be to begin sharing their faith, or perhaps getting involved in a ministry to serve the needs of others. Eventually, as the four-generation model of 2 Timothy 2:2 implies, the disciple herself should be involved in making disciples. We should be making disciples who are themselves making disciples. That is part of spiritual growth.

As might be the case with parents of a twenty-five-year-old who still wants to act like a teenager, this aspect of disciple making can get uncomfortable. Note again, however, the verbs and adjectives in Paul's commands: "... entrust to reliable people who will also be qualified to teach others." For the work of disciple making to go beyond the second generation, we must choose *reliable* people to *entrust* with that gospel. They must be willing to grow and accept those challenges. The primary qualifications for being *able to teach others* are knowledge of the word, and practice of the word: "thought accompanied by endeavor."

So what if we invest in disciple making and the would-be disciple is not proving reliable? What if they aren't willing or ready to grow? This can be the uncomfortable part for the disciple maker. If the relationship isn't one that allows that "entrusting" that Paul exhorts Timothy toward, we likely need to reinvest our time. This does not mean we reject the person, or stop caring about him or her, or in any way judge the person's worth to God. It may mean, however, that in our finiteness and the finiteness of our time, and in the importance of the task of the gospel, we reinvest our disciple-making efforts in others to whom we can entrust the gospel, who will prove reliable and teachable.

This brings us back to the Scriptures. Paul describes some of the usefulness of our God-breathed Scripture in terms of "teaching, rebuking, correcting and training in righteousness." This would also be a good description of at least some important aspects of disciple making. As this passage makes clear, the word of God is central to all of these. Yet even that list, without the context of the entire letter, might give the wrong impression. In the next paragraph Paul returns to this notion of correcting and rebuking, but in his final charge he adds two more important aspects: encouraging and patience.

> 2 Preach the word; be prepared in season and out of season; correct, rebuke and encourage—with great patience and careful instruction. 3 For the time will come when people will not put up with sound doctrine. Instead, to suit their own desires, they will gather around them a great number of teachers to say what their itching ears want to hear. 4 They will turn their ears away from the truth and turn aside to myths. (2 Timothy 4:2–4, NIV).

Correct and rebuking may be important at times. And certainly the disciple maker is called to do the work of exhorting and challenging the disciple to spiritual growth toward Christian maturity. Careful instruction, especially in the word of God, is vital. Indeed, careful instruction and sound doctrine are the antidotes to the problems we described earlier and which Paul seems to be addressing in 4:3—problems that stem from bad doctrine, and from the distorting cultural lenses we all wear. Thus disciple making is—to state it once again—rooted in the word of God. The result of that work is a changing of our lenses so that we see truly.

Yet if we leave encouragement and patience out of discipleship, focusing only on correcting or rebuking, or on doctrine without love, then our efforts are likely to result in the sorts of bad experiences of "disciple making" that lead people to reject the concept of discipleship altogether. As I was writing this book, I was also helping prepare a day-long mini-conference on disciple making for my church. I asked my wife, Deborah, who has lived her adult life committed to discipleship and disciple making, to lead one of the sessions on how to challenge others to growth. As she thought about what she might say, her first thought was that challenge and exhortation in addition to biblically rooted must come out of place of love; the one being challenged must know that the one doing the challenging cares about them. And this leads us into the next chapter and a second aspect of disciple making.

3

Disciple Making and Relationship

> To Timothy, my dear son: Grace, mercy and peace from God the Father and Christ Jesus our Lord. 3 I thank God, whom I serve, as my ancestors did, with a clear conscience, as night and day I constantly remember you in my prayers. 4 Recalling your tears, I long to see you, so that I may be filled with joy.—2 Timothy 1:2-4, NIV

"YOU THEN, MY SON . . . entrust . . ." Paul writes to Timothy. To me, this English verb *entrust* implies something relational. I *entrust* something *to* a person because I have trust in that person. Whether it was the care of my children to a babysitter (in days now long past), or care of my car to a would-be borrower, that trust has been built out of relationship. The more important the thing I am entrusting, the greater the level of trust that is needed, and the more significant that relationship must be. It's not surprising, therefore, that this verb *entrust* follows closely after Paul addresses Timothy as his son (a point we will return to very shortly). The Greek word Paul uses here is the same word used by Jesus on the cross (Luke 23:46), speaking to his father, when he *commends* or *entrusts* his spirit into his Father's hands: a relationship of both perfect unity and perfect trust.

I was fortunate that my first experience with what I might call "intentional discipleship" was a positive one. It inspired in me a lifetime desire to be invested in disciple making, and provided one model of what a disciple-making relationship could look like. It began my first year of college and lasted three and a half years until my graduation. Prior to that I'd had important adult Christian figures in my life, including my parents who were instrumental in starting the lifetime process of forming me as a disciple of Christ. Freshman year of college, however, I first became a willing and eager partner in that sort of relationship that I could identify as one of discipleship—that is, as the recipient or beneficiary of disciple making.

Doug was on staff with a campus Christian ministry at the college I attended. Part of his work was meeting with students in discipleship relationships. I suppose he was a professional disciple maker. It might, therefore, have been tempting for me to dismiss the significance of our relationship as just part of his job. Yet if we take seriously the Great Commission, then *anybody* who claims to be a Christian—that is, any follower or disciple of Christ—is also given the work of making disciples every bit as much as Doug or any campus ministry worker or paid pastoral staff in a church. If you are a follower of Christ, then disciple making is part of your job also; it is in the job description given by Christ himself. In any case, I knew Doug cared about me as a person, and invested in my life. He listened to me, encouraged me, challenged me (making me uncomfortable at times, in a way I need to be uncomfortable), and just hung out with me. My favorite outings were trips in his car—I didn't have a car in college—to the next town over for the Tuesday chili dog special and root beer floats at the A&W drive-in restaurant. I could share my frustrations with him, as well as my joys. We ate meals together. He led a Bible study that I took part in, and also helped me to lead a Bible study for others. In short, he helped me mature in faith by investing his life in me in a personal, relational way.

A Dear Son

Disciple making is relational. Paul begins his second letter to Timothy addressing him as a "dear son." Like many other examples in his writing, it is a metaphorical term. Timothy was not Paul's biological son. In his earlier letter, Paul explicitly acknowledges the metaphorical (rather than biological) nature of that relationship with a qualification, addressing Timothy as "my true son *in faith*" (emphasis added). Altogether he addresses Timothy as his "son" or "child" four times in the two letters he wrote to him that survive for us today, including in 2 Timothy 2:1 at the start of the passage that is the central topic of this book: "You then, *my son*, be strong in the grace that is in Christ Jesus." Paul also mentions Timothy in the third person in letters to various churches, again referring to him as a son. In a letter to the church in Corinth, Paul refers to Timothy as "my son whom I

Disciple Making and Relationship

love" (1 Corinthians 4:17, NIV), and in his letter to the Philippian church Paul writes of Timothy, "as a son with his father he has served with me in the work of the gospel" (Philippians 2:22, NIV).

Like the best of biological parent-child relationships, theirs is a close and nurturing relationship. We see this in Paul's use of "dear"—in Greek, *agapeto*, which could also be translated as "beloved," an adjective form of the more famous noun *agape*. We see it also in Paul's expression of a longing to see Timothy; Paul mentions this longing at the start of the letter (1:4) and two more times near the end of the letter (4:9 and 4:21). We see Paul's nurturing care for Timothy in his ongoing desire for him to grow in his faith, in his fatherly and pastoral concern for Timothy's well-being expressed in his prayers (1:3), and even in his warnings (4:15). Paul knows Timothy personally; he knows Timothy's family background and his personality (1:4–5). He has been invested in Timothy's growth and training (1:6). Paul's disciple-making work in the life of Timothy was not only relational, but deeply so, with the closeness of familial relationship.

Although I've come to deeply appreciate the spiritual leadership aspect of this disciple-making relationship implied by the father-son metaphor, many Christians resist it. I wrote at the start of this chapter about Doug's disciple-making work in my life. What I didn't mention was my own attitude issues. I grew up in a Christian home, and I became a Christian at an early age. I really can't say there was a particular date in my life before which I was not a believer and follower of Christ, and after which I was. I had no conversion experience. I think as a five-year-old, I had a five-year-old's understanding of the gospel, and to the extent I understood it I put my faith in Jesus. Likewise, as an eight-year-old I had an eight-year-old's understanding and faith. One year at a summer camp, when I was maybe ten or eleven years old, I responded to an invitation to ask Christ into my life, but I did so to make the counselors feel good and not because I was making that decision for the first time. As a teenager, I chose to be baptized and made a public confession of faith in Christ at my baptism. I did that out of obedience to my understanding of Scripture, but I didn't identify that with a *recent* decision to follow Christ or with a moment of salvation; I would have said at the time of my baptism that I'd been a Christian for years. In high school, I was conscious of sharing my faith, trying to live out a consistent Christian witness (though I was far from perfect), having some sort of daily life of prayer (I was far from perfect in that, also), reading the Bible, and fellowship with other Christians.

In short, when I went off to college I thought I had things pretty well together; I viewed myself as a self-sufficient Christian ready to lead others. During my first week of college I started a freshman Bible study on campus and advertised it with some posters in a couple of dorms. Early in my life, my father had been on staff with a Christian campus ministry. Both of my older brothers had gone to college, and had been involved with that same ministry at their respective campuses. The college I attended didn't have that particular ministry with which I had grown up. It had a different one: the one that Doug was on staff with—the "competition" (so I thought). I think I went to one or two of their meetings. I went with a critical attitude looking for reasons not to like it, and not surprisingly I quickly decided I didn't need to continue. After all, I was already leading my own Bible study, with several students involved.

It's interesting in life how our own faults and bad attitudes can come back around years later. I had a prideful attitude thinking of myself as a wise, mature, eighteen-year-old college freshman who'd grown up in the church and didn't need a more mature Christian to lead me. For the past thirty-five years of my life in academia, first as a graduate student and then as a college professor, I have been involved one way or another in ministry of disciple making on college campuses, often working with a campus ministry group. In that time, I have met many students who, like the younger me, have been disdainful of the idea that one Christian might in some way lead another; that an eighteen- to twenty-one-year-old believer might benefit from a relationship with a believer who had been walking with the Lord for a few years longer; or even that a new sixty-year-old believer might grow from the mentoring and teaching of a forty-year-old believer who had been walking with the Lord for decades; that there might be something to the father-son metaphor that Paul uses to describe his relationship with Timothy. *Aren't we all just co-learners? Why do we need a leader?*

There is certainly truth in the thought that we are all brothers and sisters in Christ, co-workers as well as co-learners, walking together on the same journey. Yet it is an incomplete truth. Yes, Doug and I were co-learners and co-laborers. Even Paul and Timothy were co-learners and co-laborers. On several occasions Paul speaks to (or of) Timothy as his son, but in his letter to the Thessalonian church (making metaphorical use of another family relationship) he calls Timothy his "brother." And in the same passage, he refers to Timothy as his "co-worker in God's service in spreading the gospel of Christ" (1 Thessalonians 3:2, NIV). He also uses the "co-worker" term to describe Timothy in his letter to the Romans. So Christian disciple making does not mean one person who knows everything passing on knowledge to somebody else. A relationship that remains like that for long becomes an unhealthy one. Likewise, disciple making certainly does not mean one person trying to control the life of another under the guise of mentorship; "disciple maker" does not mean "dictator"—not even benevolent dictator. It is worth repeating: we make disciples *for* and *of* Christ, and not disciples of ourselves. Disciple making involves *mutual* discipleship of Christ.

Yet there is, in Christian disciple making—as the example of Paul and Timothy illustrates—very often an aspect of a more mature believer leading a newer or younger believer, and passing on both lifestyle and teaching like a father to a son. Putting together several passages from Acts and Paul's other epistles, John Stott offers a summary of the relationship between Paul and Timothy:

> For over 15 years, since he had first been recruited in his home town Lystra, Timothy had been Paul's faithful missionary companion. He had travelled with him throughout most of the second and third missionary journeys and had been sent during them as a trusted apostolic delegate on several special missions . . . It is not just that Paul had a strong affection for Timothy as a friend whom he had evidently led to Christ, so that he could call him his "beloved and faithful child in the Lord" (1 Cor. 4:17). It is also that he had grown to trust Timothy as his "fellow-worker" (Rom. 16:21) and his "brother and God's servant in the gospel of Christ" (1 Thess. 3:2). Indeed, because of Timothy's genuine concern for the welfare of the churches and because of the loyalty with which "as a son with a father" he had served with Paul in the gospel, Paul could go so far as to say "I have no one like him" (Phil. 2:20–22).[1]

What if Timothy, when asked to join Paul on his missionary endeavors, had refused, claiming that he didn't need a more mature Christian to teach him because he was capable of learning and growing on his own?

During Christmas break of my freshman year of college, I went to a big missions conference with about 14,000 other college students. Through challenging talks and testimonies from various missionaries and biblical teachers, I began to see my lack of humility in this regard. I think the Holy Spirit used those talks in my life, prompting me to go back to college that winter and get involved in the ministry that already existed on my campus

---

1. Stott, *The Message of 2 Timothy*, 18–19.

(rather than trying to continue as a self-sufficient loner). That soon led to the discipleship relationship with Doug. For that relationship and Doug's investment in my life—and for his patience with my pride—I remain deeply grateful. I learned a great deal from him, not only from his teaching, but also from his model of faithful obedience and humble service to Christ, and from his example of investing in my life. Though he was closer to my age than to my father's age, it would not have been inappropriate for him to call me "dear son"—though probably "obnoxious little brother" would have been more accurate.

Discipleship and Heroes of the Faith

Earlier in this book, addressing the importance of developing a moral and theological imagination, I mentioned the author Dick Keyes and some of his reflections on heroism. Though a more thorough exploration can be found in his book *True Heroism in a World of Celebrity Counterfeits*, some seeds of those ideas are found in his earlier book *Beyond Identity* (one of the most important books I've ever read). His comment is worth quoting again. "How rare," he writes, "are writers like C. S. Lewis whose genius as a writer of fiction lay in his ability to make moral goodness attractive and heroic."

Why are heroes important? Or, more specifically, why is it important to portray moral goodness as heroic? The answer is simple. Heroes inspire us. They inspire us to action. We imitate our heroes. Indeed, that is almost the *definition* of a hero: a hero is one who inspires our emulation. In particular, heroes inspire us more than abstractions and platitudes do. Heroes may *tell* us about moral goodness, but then they demonstrate that moral goodness, showing us that moral goodness is indeed heroic. And in doing so, they make that moral goodness attractive.

Almost every year, at least two of my sons attend a Comic Con convention on the east coast. They dress up as characters from a favorite movie, book, comic, television series, or other fictional universe. They walk around all day in elaborate costumes, visiting booths and displays, buying wares, and hopefully getting photos with a favorite celebrity or two—usually an actor or actress from a favorite sci-fi or fantasy film or televisions series. They don't go dressed up as an abstract principle. I've never heard one of them say, "This year I'm going dressed as 'kindness to a neighbor'" or "This year I'm going dressed as 'mercy.'" My sons would definitely acknowledge that kindness and mercy are good traits, and I've witnessed those traits at

Disciple Making and Relationship

work in their lives, but those abstract moral principles don't inspire us the same way heroes do.

Heroes engage our imagination, impacting our thoughts and behaviors at a deeper level. This is why it is very important who our heroes are—that is to say, whom we *choose* as our heroes. Those fortunate enough to have been introduced to the writings of J. R. R. Tolkien might ask WWFD: *What Would Frodo do?* As for me, I want to know what Faramir would do. One of the literary passages that has inspired me most comes from *The Lord of the Rings.* Denethor, the ruler of Gondor, rebukes his son Faramir for failing to claim the One Ring of power, saying that Faramir's "gentleness may be repaid with death." Faramir's reply is beautiful and simple: "So be it."[2] It would be better to lose the war, Faramir believes, than to win the war if winning a war causes us to give up the very moral virtues we claim to honor and desire: mercy, truthfulness, or even a seemingly simple virtue such as gentleness. Faramir's example does more to inspire those virtues in me than an abstract argument about the importance of gentleness.

Interestingly, within his works of fiction Tolkien gives indications that Frodo and Faramir were both discipled by Gandalf; their own virtues and values were shaped by Gandalf's teaching as well as his example. At the start of the tale, Frodo is slow to mercy and quick to condemn Gollum to death. Gandalf, however, demonstrates mercy and kindness. By the end of the story, thanks in no small part to Gandalf's teaching and example, a wiser Frodo is able to show mercy even to Gollum. And one of Denethor's scathing critiques of Faramir is that he is a pupil of the wizard—a critique that readers of the tale actually recognize as a sign of Faramir's wisdom. In the context of this book, we would say that Gandalf was doing the work of disciple making, and he was effective at it, thanks in no small part to the time he spent building relationships with Frodo and others.

Likewise, when the author of Hebrews seeks to explain the meaning of faith, he does so not so much by giving a definition as by giving examples. That is, he gives only a very short abstract definition, followed by a short (still somewhat abstract and impersonal) example of faith, which combined take up a mere three verses. "Now faith is confidence in what we hope for and assurance about what we do not see. This is what the ancients were commended for. By faith we understand that the universe was formed at God's command, so that what is seen was not made out of what was visible." (Hebrews 11:1–3, NIV). The remainder of the chapter, however, offers

2. Tolkien, *The Lord of the Rings,* Book I, Chapter iv.

one concrete example after another of great heroes of faith: Abel, Enoch, Noah, Abraham, Moses, etc. The author focuses on what these heroes *did*, and sometimes also on what they *thought*, and only briefly (for example in verses 13–16) explains the meaning of those actions. The author knows that examples are more valuable in teaching the meaning of faith than abstract definitions; heroes teach the meaning of faith by demonstrating a life of faith. Thus, the author of Hebrews, just a few paragraphs after this list of heroes, writes, "Remember your leaders, who spoke the word of God to you. Consider the outcome of their way of life and imitate their faith" (Hebrews 13:7, NIV). This aspect of disciple making—the modeling of faith—is most evident in relationship when we can get to know somebody well. Hebrews also reminds us of the primary principle we explored in the previous chapter, which is that discipleship must be centered on the word of God; the leaders to be imitated are the ones who both lived and spoke that word.

Of course, the ultimate hero for all Christians should be Christ himself. He is the one we should imitate. We should be making disciples of Christ and not ourselves. The reason Paul as disciple maker is a model for others—one to be imitated—is because he himself imitates Christ. "Follow my example, as I follow the example of Christ," he writes to the church in Corinth (1 Corinthians 11:1). "We did this," he writes to the church in Thessalonica (to explain why he accepted no financial support from them) "not because we do not have the right to such help, but in order to offer ourselves as a *model* for you to *imitate*" (2 Thessalonians 3:9, NIV, emphasis added).

And this example of Paul offering himself up as one to be imitated brings us back to Paul and his second epistle to Timothy.

Way of Life, Purpose, Faith, Patience, Love, Endurance

As Paul approaches the end of his letter and his final charge—just before his famous passage about the usefulness of Scripture for teaching and training, and just after stating how difficult times will be for followers of Christ—he offers another personal note of encouragement to Timothy.

> 10 You, however, know all about my teaching, my way of life, my purpose, faith, patience, love, endurance, 11 persecutions, sufferings—what kinds of things happened to me in Antioch, Iconium and Lystra, the persecutions I endured. Yet the Lord rescued me

Disciple Making and Relationship

> from all of them. 12 In fact, everyone who wants to live a godly life in Christ Jesus will be persecuted, 13 while evildoers and impostors will go from bad to worse, deceiving and being deceived. (2 Timothy 3:10–13, NIV)

Yes, as he notes here, Paul has passed on his *teaching*: his testimony rooted in the gospel that we described in the previous chapter. You don't need to read very far in any of Paul's letters to realize that Paul works hard to teach sound doctrine. This is important, of course. So important that it is worth repeating often. Discipleship is rooted in the word of God. But more than that, Paul has also passed on his very life. Because discipleship is relational.

Notice what comes after "teaching" in the list of what Timothy knows about Paul: "way of life," "purpose," "faith," "patience," "love," "endurance," "persecutions," "sufferings." Not one of the things on this list can reduced to an abstraction. None of these are simply doctrines that can be correctly handled. Timothy can know these things about Paul only by having witnessed them, because he was so often with Paul, because the disciple-making relationship is a personal relationship that takes place over time: an investment of one's life and not just a passing on of ideas. Eugene Peterson's translation in *The Message* captures this beautifully:

> You've been a good apprentice to me, a part of my teaching, my manner of life, direction, faith, steadiness, love, patience, troubles, sufferings—suffering along with me in all the grief I had to put up with in Antioch, Iconium, and Lystra. And you also well know that God rescued me! Anyone who wants to live all out for Christ is in for a lot of trouble; there's no getting around it. Unscrupulous con men will continue to exploit the faith. They're as deceived as the people they lead astray. As long as they are out there, things can only get worse. (2 Timothy 3:10–13, MSG)

Paul can write with assurance to Timothy, "you also know well that God rescued me!" He can write that because Timothy spent so much time with Paul, not just listening to teaching, but working with him, following him, helping him. Timothy witnessed Paul's life firsthand, from up close.

This passing on of one's life, and living out one's teaching in a visible and vulnerable way, is especially important (as Paul notes here) because the life committed to discipleship is not always easy. Indeed, for Paul (as well as many other disciples of Christ) there seem to have been very few moments that could be described as "easy." Having lived my entire life in a wealthy country with religious freedom, I've never had to endure the sorts of things

Paul had to endure: the troubles, suffering, and grief he put up with at Antioch, Iconium, and Lystra, or the other troubles he will mention later in the chapter. Remember that Paul wrote this letter while in prison awaiting his execution having been sentenced to death by Nero. Early church documents suggest that Paul was beheaded on the same day that Peter was executed by being hanged upside down on a cross. Paul, when he was still named Saul, also witnessed the stoning (to death) of Stephen. I, by contrast, write this book sitting in a comfortable house drinking a cup of tea and eating crackers with homemade jam that my wife just brought me. I think of Paul's words to Timothy, "Everyone who wants to live a godly life in Christ Jesus will be persecuted." The hostility I face for my faith is exceedingly mild compared to what Paul faced—or what was endured by most of the heroes of faith listed in Hebrews 11, or even what is endured by Christians today in many parts of the world. And yet it is still a temptation for me to compromise my faith in order to avoid even those few mild instances of what might be called "persecution."

Earlier in this book, I warned about what is often called fear-mongering: an effort to stir up fear in others in order to get them to act in a certain way (to avoid whatever they are afraid of), or more often in order to get them to give money to a cause so that the purveyors of fear (who are often also the collectors of contributions) can fight some battle against the supposed danger. The church has often been guilty of this sort of fear-mongering. *The big bad world outside the church wants to harm Christians. Don't let this happen. Give to our cause. Make sure a certain person doesn't get elected, because if that person gets elected then Christians will be in trouble and our way of life will end and the church will collapse. Etc.* This isn't a new phenomenon, though it seems to have intensified in recent years. On July 7, 1995, in an insightful *Calvin and Hobbes* comic, author Bill Waterson depicts this fundraising strategy through the character of Calvin, who explains how to use fear and antagonism in order to get donations. The particular highlighted fear to be exploited is an attack on values. It is all too familiar—and, unfortunately, familiar even (or perhaps especially) within the church.[3]

It is easy to give in to this way of thinking: to get caught up by the threats and live in fear. This is especially true if we have been deceived by prosperity gospel into thinking that health and wealth is a right—an

---

3. Bill Waterson, "Calvin and Hobbes," July 7, 1995, www.gocomics.com/calvinandhobbes/1995/07/07, accessed October 11, 2019.

expectation that all Christians should be able to have. If I think I somehow deserve these things because of my faith, then I am more prone to give in to fear when the fear-mongers come along claiming that somebody is trying to take them away from me.

Consider, however, a few observations from Paul's letter to Timothy. Yes, Paul issues several warnings to Timothy—at least one in each of the final three chapters of this letter. However, nearly all of these warnings (2 Timothy 2:17–18; 3:1–9; 4:3–4) are about bad teaching *within* the church: about religious people offering us false doctrines or *un*-biblical messages. The only significant warning against a threat from outside the church is about Alexander the metalworker who did some harm to Paul (4:14). And even in the warning about Alexander, Paul resists fear-mongering threats that all of God's work will be futile if Alexander is left to continue his opposition; rather, Paul points out (4:17–18) that God never abandoned him: that God still stood by Paul's side and strengthened him, delivering him from "the lion's mouth," and most importantly that God's work was still accomplished: the gospel was fully proclaimed despite the opposition.

This is not the first time Paul shares this message even within this short letter. What he demonstrates through his own life witness, he has already explicitly stated to Timothy earlier in the letter: Christians will be persecuted, as Paul has been, but that persecution is not somehow going to destroy the church or halt God's work and witness. Paul may be suffering in chains like a criminal, he tells Timothy, but God's word is *not* chained (2:9). False teachers may depart from the truth and lead others astray, but the solid foundation of the gospel and the word of God will stand firm (2:17–19). If our big concern is to avoid hardship, to live comfortable lives as nice churchgoing people, then this message might be discouraging. But for those whose biggest hope and joy is the work of the gospel, the making of disciples, then these words are wonderfully encouraging. When we understand "church" to be those carrying out God's kingdom work of disciple making on earth (and not a financial or social organization), then we realize that the greatest threat to the church isn't persecution from outside, but rather a bad witness that results from moral compromise or a failure to follow God. Paul's words make that clear, as does the witness of his life. God's word isn't going to be chained or imprisoned. (Indeed, plenty of evidence suggests it thrives most in the midst of persecution.) Christians do not need to pursue political, financial, cultural, or military power in order to protect

God's word. To the contrary, the pursuit of those things may be the biggest threat to the extent that they harm the witness of the church.

This idea is so important in Paul's writing, and in biblical teaching in general—and the temptation to act out of fear is so pervasive in the contemporary church—that it is worth considering further. I'm normally wary of just looking at isolated verses as it is too easy to take them out of context, but certain topics are addressed so often in Scripture that sometimes it is a worthwhile exercise. So consider how often the Bible encourages, exhorts, or commands God's followers not to be a afraid. If you have never done so, take a few minutes and search an online NIV Bible for the phrases: "Do not be afraid," "Do not fear," and "Do not be terrified." Actually, it will take more than a few minutes to read them all. When you are done, take a little more time to meditate on some of the antidotes or opposites of fear, such as courage; consider biblical commands to have courage or be courageous, such as the numerous Old Testament uses of the phrase, "Be strong and courageous." After you have taken the time to do this, the picture should be clear enough without more work, but go ahead anyway and spend some time considering Jesus' teaching on "worry" (especially in Matthew 6 and Luke 12) and Paul's teaching about "anxiety" (Philippians 4:6)—two concepts very close to fear. The overall biblical message might be summarized best in Psalm 27, which begins with the rhetorical questions: "The Lord is my light and my salvation—whom shall I fear? The Lord is the stronghold of my life—of whom shall I be afraid?" (Psalm 27:1, NIV). The psalmist David—who from a human standpoint had many reasons over the course of his life to be afraid—almost immediately answers his own questions: "Though an army besiege me, my heart will not fear; though war break out against me, even then I will be confident" (Psalm 27:3, NIV).

Now turn back to 2 Timothy. Although Paul doesn't use explicitly use the word *fear*, he does remind Timothy not to be *timid*. Yes, Timothy will experience persecution. So will all who seek to follow Christ, as Paul repeatedly makes clear. Yet his message to Timothy isn't about how to avoid persecution or suffering; it is a message to continue the proclamation of the gospel and the work of disciple making even in the midst of persecution and suffering, without compromising his faith or the gospel upon which that faith is based.

The following seems clear, then: the message "be afraid" is un-biblical. That is to say, the message "fear the Lord" is sound biblical teaching. Any other message of fear is not. So when somebody tells you to be

Disciple Making and Relationship

afraid—whether in an appeal to elicit a contribution (out of fear) or to vote a certain way (out of fear)—recognize that it is not the Bible speaking.

More broadly, I believe it is a temptation for many Christians in this country to compromise integrity, morality, and truth-speaking in order to avoid persecution or discomfort. To gain political power that might prevent some opposition, we make compromises that can often severely damage the witness of the church. How important it is, therefore, to have models of disciple makers willing to endure hardship for the sake of the gospel.

For Paul's example doesn't end with himself, or even with Timothy. Remember the four generations of believers in his letter? What Paul passes on to Timothy, Timothy should pass on to faithful followers, who themselves should teach others. That's the nature of disciple making. And as important as it is to be centered on the word of God, and to handle that word correctly, this passing on of the gospel depends not just on teaching but on lived example and thus on relationships. So Paul could confidently write the following words to the church in Corinth: "Therefore I urge you to imitate me. For this reason I have sent to you Timothy, my son whom I love, who is faithful in the Lord. He will remind you of my way of life in Christ Jesus, which agrees with what I teach everywhere in every church" (1 Corinthians 4:16–17, NIV). There, once again, is the call to imitate. Paul has sought to imitate Christ: to root his "way of life in Christ" so that his life and teaching are consistent, and in agreement. The church at Corinth can therefore imitate Paul's model, his Christ-rooted "way of life," which they know because Paul has spent time with them. They need only be reminded of what they have witnessed in his life, and heard in his teaching. And, moreover, since Paul has lived out his witness with Timothy, he can send Timothy to Corinth and the church there can learn from Timothy, who has imitated Paul, who has imitated Christ. This requires that Timothy spend time with them in relationship, modeling the sort of teaching and behavior that the disciples of Christ should imitate.

4

Disciple Making and Christian Community

> And the things you have heard me say *in the presence of many witnesses* entrust to reliable people who will also be qualified to teach others.
>
> —2 Timothy 2:2, NIV, emphasis added

Two cultural lenses prevalent in the United States during my lifetime in the late twentieth and early twenty-first centuries are the distorting lenses of *consumerism* and *individualism*. The two are closely related. If, for example, you view church through the lens of individualism, your expectation may be that church exists to meet some personal desire such as finding spiritual fulfillment. When you view church with this purpose in mind, you will evaluate a church based on how it fulfills that personal desire; you will view church as a product, and yourself as a consumer of that product shopping for the best option. Which is to say, you will also view church through a lens of consumerism, and churches in turn will need to compete for customers just like businesses in our consumerist society.

So consumerism and individualism go hand in hand. Both are also central aspects of our culture. If you are reading this book, it's likely difficult for you not to see through those lenses. Removing those lenses and seeing instead through the lens of biblical faith and a resurrection gospel requires effort and intention. That's why I wrote earlier about the danger of spending eight (or more) hours a week consuming media—even or perhaps especially news media—while spending a fraction of that time actively engaged in Scripture. If this is your pattern, then you can't help but see the world and even the Bible itself through the distorting lens of your favorite media, all the advertisements that fund it, and all the other trappings of our modern Western culture.

We will explore the impacts of the lens of consumerism in chapter 6. In this chapter, we focus on individualism. The lens of individualism tells us a couple things. First, it tells us that our own personal fulfillment or happiness is the highest goal. Seen through the lens of individualism, the goal of a job is finding personal fulfillment, the goal of getting married or having family is personal fulfillment, and even the goal of going church or becoming a Christian is to find personal fulfillment. We slide toward the false message of the feel-good prosperity gospel. Or church becomes a type of therapy and we replace the Christian gospel with a moralistic therapeutic deism. As I mentioned in my introduction, the death of my nephew revealed ways that this false message had crept into my own heart. That lens has us asking questions like, "Did that worship service make me feel good?"—which may be thinly disguised as a question like, "Did that worship service help me personally experience God?" We shop for jobs or spouses or churches or even religions the way we would shop for a car or a breakfast cereal or a new pair of jeans. At its most blunt, individualism tells us, *It's all about me.*

A second aspect of this lens of individualism is the value placed on self-sufficiency and independence: it is better not to rely upon or need anybody else. I grew up with movies from the 1970s and 1980s—and plenty of replayed films of the 1950s and 1960s. The archetypal heroes of these films included James Bond as well as various characters played by John Wayne (in Westerns and war movies alike). In the 1970s, an archetypal police officer hero was provided by Clint Eastwood's "Dirty" Harry Callahan. For nearly thirty years starting in 1982, Sylvester Stallone's Rambo offered yet another standard soldier-hero-loner. Despite the occasional token effort made to show these characters getting help from somebody, what they generally had in common was an ability to handle things on their own, and often a disdain for help. Even soldiers depicted in many war films were often loners. Despite occasional modern films that team superheroes together in loose affiliations (Marvel's *Avengers* or DC's *Justice League*), most of the spate of commercially successful superhero films over the past few decades have focused on a self-sufficient super-powered individual solving the world's problems. In today's culture, being self-sufficient is often the definition of a hero.

However, if we look through a biblical lens—and if we examine a biblical model of discipleship and disciple making—we see things rather differently.

In the Presence of Many Witnesses

Disciple making happens in the context of community. Although this third principle of disciple making may be less obvious in 2 Timothy than the principles outlined in the previous two chapters, it is no less important and it is certainly suggested. If we expand our exploration behind Paul's letter to include other New Testament writings—including Paul's other epistles as well as the teachings of Jesus—then this principle becomes even more pronounced.

We can begin by looking right back at 2 Timothy 2:2, and the second phrase of that sentence: "in the presence of many witnesses." The word witnesses—*marturon* in the Greek, which is related to our modern word *martyr*—is used often in the New Testament. One of my favorite examples is Hebrews 12:1, which refers to the heroes of the faith described in Hebrews 11 as a "great cloud of witnesses." The word can be used in a legal sense to describe a witness in a trial, or it could refer to a witness of a historical event. The term also took a particular meaning in the Christian church to refer to one who bore witness to Christ by giving his or her life for the sake of the gospel, such as Stephen: a martyr in the modern sense. John Stott suggests that Paul uses the term "witnesses" in his letter to Timothy to emphasize the trustworthiness of his message; it wasn't passed on in secret but rather in front of others who could attest to Paul's words. Stott writes:

> And the reference to many witnesses shows that the apostolic faith was not a secret tradition handed on privately to Timothy ... whose authenticity there was no means of testing, but a public instruction, whose truth was guaranteed by the many witnesses who had heard it and could therefore check Timothy's teaching against the apostle's.[1]

---

1. Stott, *The Message of 2 Timothy*, 50–51.

Disciple Making and Christian Community

Stott also points out that the Greek tense in the previous phrase makes it clear that Paul is not writing about a "single public occasion" of his teaching, but "rather to the totality of his instruction over the years."[2] My first point though, is a somewhat simpler one. Paul's disciple-making work in the life of Timothy takes place in the context of community. His teaching, in particular, took place in the presence of many witnesses.

There are several important reasons why community is important in discipleship and disciple making. At least a few are suggested here as it relates to teaching. First, having an important component of our teaching and exploration of Scripture take place in the context of community is one of the safeguards against heresy. Others besides Timothy can hear what Paul says to Timothy. When we do the teaching work of disciple making within community, it becomes at least possible for others to question our words—for example, if we say something inconsistent with the words of Jesus, or with the gospel message, or with other Scriptures, or simply if we say something that might be misunderstood. To put this another way, community provides a level of accountability for the teacher. Paul might be saying something like, *I was never trying to deceive you, Timothy; others heard what I had to say.* Of course, the other witnesses could also see Paul's behavior as well as hear his teaching, and so it provides a double layer of accountability that is not present when disciple making is a private matter. Abuse is still possible even within a community, but the witnesses of community provide a level of safeguard.

Paul brings home the importance of community and of sound teaching (being rooted in the word of God, properly taught) in the following paragraphs when he gives two warnings to Timothy. One warning is about the damage caused by false teachers who "have departed from the truth." These false teachings, Paul tells Timothy (using yet another metaphor), can "spread like gangrene" and "destroy the faith of some" (2 Timothy 2:17–18, NIV). Another set of warnings is against quarreling. In 2:14 Paul instructs Timothy to warn his congregation against quarreling, which (like false doctrine) can prove ruinous. And again in 2:23–24 he warns against "foolish and stupid arguments," which might lead to quarrels, which God's servant—the disciple and disciple maker of Christ—should not get involved with. Other than the fact that the quarrels can be ruinous, Paul does not give any detail about *why* they are bad. However, at least one answer seems obvious to me: quarrels tear apart communities, and Paul makes it clear

---

2. Stott, *The Message of 2 Timothy*, 50.

that community is vitally important to the work of disciple making. One antidote to quarreling is good teaching along with the practice of kindness and gentleness (2:24–25), which build community, and indeed are at the core of the relational and Bible-centered work we explored in the previous two chapters.

Likewise, this community of believers who heard Paul's words can also help make sure Timothy is passing that teaching on correctly to others. As Stott noted, these other witnesses "could therefore check Timothy's teaching against the apostle's." A community of believers is also a wonderful context for studying Scripture together, as each can gain from the experience, wisdom, and insights of others. Scripture is challenging. It is not just difficult at times to apply; it can be difficult even to understand. Although it may at first seem ironic, a small *group* Bible study is one of the best settings or contexts for one-on-one relational disciple making. Even when there is a leader, all members of the group are still co-learners together. For example, earlier in the book I mentioned that there are some passages whose meaning is clearly metaphorical. Even when we know the author is speaking in metaphor, we still wrestle together using our imaginations and knowledge of Scripture to unravel that metaphor. Other times, a literal translation is clear from context, and even then we still wrestle to understand the implications. In some instances between those extremes, we may have to struggle to understand whether a teaching was meant literally or metaphorically. While there is an important purpose for *personal* study and meditation on Scripture, there is also an important purpose for this sort of *communal* aspect of the work of disciple making.

A Body, A Building, A Family, A Nation

All of this begins to get at the importance of community in discipleship, and why disciple making happens in the context of the church. Yet we have so far looked only at the fringes of a wide tapestry of community. The importance of the fellowship and community of the Christian church is absolutely central to Christian discipleship. Consider that several of the most prominent New Testament metaphors describing life in Christ have to do with unity and community of all believers. The authors and teachers of the New Testaments describes the church—that is, the collection of Christ's followers—variously as a *body*, a *building*, a *family*, and a *nation*.

Disciple Making and Christian Community

Paul develops the metaphor of body in his letter to the Romans (Romans 12:4–10) and in even greater depth in the first of his surviving letters to the Corinthian church (1 Corinthians 12:4–30). He returns to the metaphor yet again in Ephesians, where the image of the church as a body runs throughout much of the letter, and then again in Colossians (1:18). To say it is an important metaphor to Paul would be an understatement. We will turn to Ephesians soon, but first consider one simple statement from each of the first two epistles mentioned above: "So in Christ we, though many, form one body, and each member belongs to all the others" Paul writes (Romans 12:5, NIV); and, again, "Just as a body, though one, has many parts, but all its many parts form one body, so it is with Christ" (1 Corinthians 12:12, NIV). Many sermons and entire books have been devoted to these passages, and rightly so. The disciple of Christ—that is, the one who claims to be "in Christ" or "with Christ"—is simply not given an option of living individually, independently, or self-sufficiently. To be in Christ is to make our gifts available to the body, and to avail ourselves of the gifts of the rest of the body, that we might grow as Christ's disciples and work as his disciple makers. Disciple making happens in the context of Christian community, which is compared to a body—a single, cohesive, unified whole, which is both the sum of all its parts and dependent on all those parts, and in which each part is dependent upon the whole.

So it is also with the other metaphors. Paul also speaks of Christians collectively as part of a building. In his first epistle to the Corinthian church he writes, "For we are co-workers in God's service; you are God's field, God's building. By the grace God has given me, I laid a foundation as a wise builder, and someone else is building on it. But each one should build with care. For no one can lay any foundation other than the one already laid, which is Jesus Christ" (1 Corinthians 3:9–11, NIV). Discipleship is not done by individual workers laboring alone, but in collaboration; like being part of a body, being "co-workers in God's service" is not something disciple makers are allowed to opt out of; we *are* that; it is part of our being in Christ, just as the foundation, walls, roofs, floors, windows, and doors are all part of a single building.

So, too, are all disciples of Christ part of a single family. If we consider, in addition to the term *family* itself, all the many family relationship terms used—son, daughter, brother, sister, father, mother—then this is the most oft-used metaphor in the New Testament. Jesus himself repeatedly uses metaphors of family to describe the relationships of his followers and disciple makers. So does Paul in several of his epistles. (See, for example, Galatians 6:10, 1 Thessalonians 4:10, and Hebrews 2:11.) The Apostle Peter uses the term *family* twice in his first general epistle (1 Peter 2:17; 5:9) to describe the community of believers, as well as the terms *brothers* and *sisters* to refer to specific Christians. Again, we can observe that following Christ is done as part of this family. Like our biological families, we aren't free to choose who our family members are. And, indeed, though followers of Christ have an obligation to do good to all, Paul notes that we have a particular obligation to do good to our family of believers (Galatians 6:10).

One other metaphor used by both Paul and Peter is also worth mentioning before we delve more deeply into Ephesians and the implications of all these metaphors for Christian disciple making. Both Peter and Paul speak of Christ's followers collectively forming a new nation, each disciple being a citizen of that nation. Though Paul doesn't use the term *nation* in Ephesians 2:12–19, he does use the metaphor, implying a nation of God when he writes of our "citizenship" and the "covenants of promise" (NIV) that comes as the rights of citizens. Indeed, Paul turns it into an even more powerful metaphor than a mere nation (such as Israel or Rome), speaking of an entire "new humanity" that Christ is making of us. Similarly, in an oft-cited passage, Peter writes, "But you are a chosen people, a royal priesthood, a holy nation, God's special possession, that you may declare the praises of him who called you out of darkness into his wonderful light" (1 Peter 2:9, NIV). This would be a potent enough metaphor for the people of Israel, who had been a literal earthly nation for many years, coming out of captivity to Egypt, being restored from yet another captivity to Babylon, and at the time of this letter still holding a sense of national identity even while living in captivity to Rome. But Paul and Peter speak not of a fleeting earthly nation, but rather use that metaphor to speak instead of a permanent spiritual nation: a nation of Christ-followers, of disciples and disciple makers. How much more powerful the idea that we are not individuals wandering the world, but citizens of an eternal kingdom with both privileges and responsibilities associated with that citizenship.

The point of dwelling on all of this is simple: to push back against the distorting cultural lenses of individualism, autonomy, and self-sufficiency. However popular and compelling that way of thinking is in our culture, it is simply not a biblical way of looking at the church, or the Christian faith, or (to the point of this book) the work of disciple making. And to that

Disciple Making and Christian Community

end, let's turn more carefully to Paul's expanding on this in his epistle to Ephesians.

The Building Up of the Whole Body

After using both the *building* and *nation-citizenship* metaphors to speak of Christ's followers (Ephesians 2) and before using the *family* metaphor of "brothers" and "sisters" (Ephesians 6), Paul expands on the metaphor of Christians (plural) as part of a body (singular) of Christ:

> 11 So Christ himself gave the apostles, the prophets, the evangelists, the pastors and teachers, 12 to equip his people for works of service, so that the body of Christ may be built up 13 until we all reach unity in the faith and in the knowledge of the Son of God and become mature, attaining to the whole measure of the fullness of Christ.
>
> 14 Then we will no longer be infants, tossed back and forth by the waves, and blown here and there by every wind of teaching and by the cunning and craftiness of people in their deceitful scheming. 15 Instead, speaking the truth in love, we will grow to become in every respect the mature body of him who is the head, that is, Christ. 16 From him the whole body, joined and held together by every supporting ligament, grows and builds itself up in love, as each part does its work. (Ephesians 4:11–16, NIV)

I subscribe to a series of daily devotions called "Life for Leaders" published by the Fuller Seminary De Pree Center. A short devotion arrives each morning in my email in-box, usually an hour or two before I awake. Mark Roberts writes the devotions on weekdays. For several months in 2018, he worked slowly, deeply, and systematically through the book of Ephesians—a series he continued into 2019. In December of 2018, he came to the passage above from Ephesians 4. Consider what he observes, in a devotion appropriately titled "It's Not Just About You":

> When we think about growing up, we tend to envision our own, individual growth. That's only natural. Similarly, when we think about growing up as Christians, we also tend to focus on our own spiritual growth. That's also only natural.
>
> It's good, but it isn't enough. Yes, as individuals we should grow up in Christ. [However,] our individual growth turns out to be essentially connected to the growth of the Christian community.

> Ephesians 4:11–16 makes it abundantly clear that in the matter of Christian growth, it's not just about you.[3]

I highly recommend Roberts's devotions in general, his series on Ephesians in particular, and even more particularly the devotions on this passage from Ephesians 4. I could quote from them at length. For now, consider his concluding paragraph of this devotion, with the idea that the growing up he speaks of—our "growth in Christ"—is the goal of disciple making.

> Therefore, though we are right to want to grow up as individual Christians (see Colossians 1:28), full Christian maturity necessarily includes the growth of the body of Christ. Once again, when it comes to growing up in Christ, it's not just about you. Your growth matters and so does that of the church. In fact, your growth in Christ is deeply entwined with the growth of your church and vice versa. You won't grow to be all that God envisions you to be apart from Christian community. And the church won't grow to be all that God envisions it to be apart from your contribution.[4]

At the start of this chapter, I stated that disciple making happens in the context of community. Narrowly understood, this might mean that my individual work of discipleship—both *being* a disciple and *making* disciples, which I claimed are part of the same work—is dependent on the church: on fellowship with and support of other believers. This is true enough. And if we look through the lens of individualism, we might even stop there. However the message of this passage is far deeper. That is to say, the importance of community in discipleship is greater even than this. Not only does the growth toward maturity of the individual disciple happen within the body, but the spiritual growth of the entire body is important. Even if we acknowledge the importance of the body, if we still view the growth of the individual as the ultimate end, then we are looking through the wrong lens. The body—the community of the church—is not only the context or *means* of discipleship, but it is also its *end*. We might say that the growth of the community that is the church and also body, building, family, and nation of God is the very goal of disciple making.

Let's put this in a broader context. Seeing Christianity through the lens of individualism, we often place a stress on a "personal relationship with God through Jesus Christ." The idea of a personal relationship with God is not in and of itself false; it is important and true. Yet it is also incomplete.

3. Roberts, "It's Not Just About You."
4. Roberts, "It's Not Just About You."

Disciple Making and Christian Community

Yes, we can talk directly to God. He knows us personally. Christ is our mediator, and the only mediator we need. That is wonderful news, indeed! I am invited to address God as "Father." What joyous intimacy! But we are not called to be in *merely* a personal relationship. That is never offered as an option to the Christian. We can't do without the church as though we don't need it, or it doesn't need us. In that sense, our relationship with God may be *personal*, but it is not *individual* at all.

Listen to this again: we are called to be part of a body, a family, a building, a nation. When we enter a relationship with Christ we *are* part of each of those (though many folks who claim to be Christians don't live that out). Just as discipleship must be rooted in the gospel, and in the word of truth that comes to us in Scripture, so it might also be lived out both *in the context* of, and also *for the purpose of*, the community that is God's body, the church.

I end this section with one more quote from Mark Roberts in a later devotion in the same series on Ephesians 4:11–16—one that connects this all to the idea of disciple maker as mentor:

> It would be wrong, however, to pit corporate growth against individual growth. Both are essential and, in fact, both depend on each other. This is implied in Ephesians 4:11–16, where the development of the church depends on actions of individual Christians. If solitary believers are not growing, then surely the growth of the whole body will be hampered.
>
> Similarly, your individual growth in Christ depends, to a great extent, on your growing Christian community. If you are in a place where others serve, teach, encourage, challenge, and pray for you, then it's likely you are growing in Christ. If you are in a church where you can watch the lives of mature believers, and where these believers mentor those who are less mature, then chances are good you'll grow to be like them.[5]

Conclusions: Truth, Relationship, Community

In 2 Timothy 2:1–2, we see these three aspects that are all vital to disciple making as part of true discipleship to Christ: it is rooted in the word of God, and especially the gospel; it is relational; it takes place in community. These are biblical principles reflected many places in Scripture, but stated especially concisely in Paul's final letter.

5. Roberts, "Growing Up is a Shared Experience."

Interestingly, before I observed these three principles in 2 Timothy 2, I saw them in another context. Steven Garber, in his important and compelling book *The Fabric of Faithfulness*, writes about the challenges faced by young men and woman coming into adulthood, navigating their twenties and thirties. Those are years full of challenges and discouragement that come with the facing of real life. Sadly, many who had been followers of Christ fall away from God during that time. Yet Garber also mentions that along with those who seem to give up or lose their way, there are others "who come through that crucible with habits of heart and mind so in place that they move on into responsibilities and privilege of adulthood without compromising their basic integrity or giving in to . . . cynicism." He goes on to wonder and explore what it is that "so forms their vision and virtues that they make it through . . . their twenties and thirties with their convictions and character intact."[6]

I have highly recommended Garber's book to many, and here I will highlight his conclusion: what has made the difference in the lives of those who have come through the crucible of those years with their faith not merely intact but thriving, who have a "vision of integrity which coherently connects belief to behavior personally as well as publicly." I don't need to give a spoiler alert. Garber himself gives the conclusion away in the introduction to this book. There are three features in particular he has observed:

> It is those who develop a worldview that can address the challenges of coherence and truth in a pluralist society, who find relationship with a mentor who incarnates that worldview, and who choose to live their lives among others whose common life is an embodiment of that worldview who continue on with integrity into adulthood.[7]

Garber's conclusions were drawn from personal relationships, history, study, and interviews. I thought of his book as I was writing this book, and it dawned on me how similar his conclusion was to the three characteristics of disciple making present in 2 Timothy 2:2. The worldview we need to develop is developed by learning to look at the world through the lens of Scripture. Indeed, the lens of God's word may be the best definition of a true worldview. It is certainly one that is coherent and true. But a casual half-hearted, pseudo-knowledge of the word won't do. Just knowing a few passages we can quote (or misquote, perhaps with little context) is

---

6. Garber, *The Fabric of Faithfulness*, 20–21.
7. Garber, *The Fabric of Faithfulness*, 20–21.

Disciple Making and Christian Community

not sufficient to address the challenges of our society. Nor will it protect us from the misquotes or misunderstandings of the word that would manipulate or confuse is. We need to study the word deeply, the difficult and confusing as well as the encouraging and easier passages, and we need to see it lived out in others. This is how the worldview is developed.

As for the need for mentors who incarnate that worldview, that is a wonderful description of the relational aspect of disciple making: both seeking out mentors and also offering ourselves as mentors who strive both to teach and to live out that worldview so that we are able to say what Paul wrote to Timothy: *You have heard my teaching and witnessed my way of life.* And lastly, we need to live our lives among others whose common life is to be disciples and disciple makers in the community of disciples and disciple makers. That is, we need to live as part of the body, the family, the building, the kingdom that we were made to be a part of, both offering our gifts in service and benefiting from the gifts of those around us.

A few pages later, Garber writes, "Weaving together belief and behavior during the university years is no small thing. And yet in every generation lovers of Christ have given heart, soul, mind and strength to the task."[8] Those words are true, and not just of university years. Discipleship including the work of disciple making may begin any time in life, and should continue to the end.

---

8. Garber, *The Fabric of Faithfulness*, 21.

5

Three Metaphors for Disciple Making

> You see, God hasn't promised you a good job or great kids. He hasn't promised you an easy marriage and a comfortable place to live. He hasn't promised you physical health and a good church to attend. He hasn't promised that you would experience affluence and be surrounded by things that entertain you. What he has promised is that he will complete the work that he has begun in you.[1]
>
> —Paul David Tripp

NEITHER JESUS IN HIS post-resurrection Great Commission to his disciples, nor Paul in his pre-execution exhortation to Timothy—a commission very similar to, and seemingly inspired by the Great Commission—make any promise that a life of disciple making will be easy. Joyful? Yes. Worthwhile? Absolutely. Although disciple making has its challenges as well as moments of discouragement, it is also often exciting, enjoyable, and full of delight. But not easy.

Early in this book, I mentioned the summer I felt an uncomfortable challenge to join some others on a short time summer mission trip to an eastern European country, one that had been closed to the gospel at the

---

1. Tripp, *Awe*, 121.

Three Metaphors for Disciple Making

time. On the final week of that life-changing summer trip, I injured my hand on a piece of broken and dirty glass. The wound went deep, completely severing a nerve leading to one of my fingers, but the real problem was the infection that set in. Medical help was not available to us in that country, and it was a couple of days before I was able to get by train across Europe to a hospital back in Austria. By then my hand was swollen like a grapefruit with tinges of pale green. I was in grave risk of losing my hand.

As I traveled by tram across the city of Vienna from the hotel where our missions group had its debrief to the hospital, I remember praying fervently for healing. All sorts of things in my life, from playing musical instruments, to competitive sports, to my passion for fishing, all made significant use of my hand. The answer I heard from God during that time of prayer, however, was not assurance that he would heal my hand. That was the answer I hoped for. What I sensed God telling me instead was that he would continue to be with me whether my hand healed or not. Neither his power in my life, nor my relationship with him, depended on that hand. I had no promise from God of health and prosperity. What I had from God was a promise of his presence and love, and his continued work in my life.

Paul David Tripp points out something similar in his book on *Awe*, noting not only that God doesn't promise us comfort, but that he doesn't even promise us a "good church to attend." What he does promise is to complete his work in his: a work of making us disciples. He also calls us to be a part of this disciple-making work. And *work* is a good term for it. As I noted earlier, the work of disciple making is no easier than Hannah's vision in the movie *Silverado* for the hard work of caring for the beautiful land where she hoped to settle. It isn't surprising that her would-be suitor Paden turned away almost immediately upon realizing what Hannah wanted, and he chose instead the life of the saloon.

That many who begin following Christ soon make a choice similar to Paden's is sad but not surprising. The disciple maker faces not only the hard work of cultivating soil, planting seed, and harvesting, but also opposition from those who have a different vision for the land. The cattle rancher McKendrick (played by Ray Baker) and his corrupt lackey Sheriff Cobb (played by Brian Dennehy) were intent on driving Hannah and her people off the land, and destroying her vision for a fruitful land. Those intent on working the land face a tough battle—quite literally at times.

In the face of that opposition and the demands of joyful but oft-challenging work, the disciple maker must bring to the task a particular set of attitudes and practices. Thus Paul follows up his concise charge in 2 Timothy 2:1–2 with three insightful metaphors. Whereas the exhortation in verse 2 is written in literal prescriptive language that engages the will through what we might refer to as the rational mind, the verses that following engage the imagination. That is to say, they provide images that offer both instruction and inspiration for those who want to live out the Great Commission of disciple making.

Consider that three-metaphor passage from Paul's letter:

> 3 Join with me in suffering, like a good soldier of Christ Jesus. 4 No one serving as a soldier gets entangled in civilian affairs, but rather tries to please his commanding officer. 5 Similarly, anyone who competes as an athlete does not receive the victor's crown except by competing according to the rules. 6 The hardworking farmer should be the first to receive a share of the crops. 7 Reflect on what I am saying, for the Lord will give you insight into all this. (2 Timothy 2:3–7, NIV)

Before reading further, take some time to dwell on these metaphors. Sit back and imagine a Roman soldier, an Olympic athlete, and a farmer tilling and planting a field (without any modern machinery). Even for Paul, whose writing is often rich with imagery, offering three metaphors in a row back-to-back-to-back is a lot. As I write this, I'm hard-pressed to think of any other passage in Scripture in which a single idea is presented with three consecutive metaphors—unless perhaps it is times when Jesus presented a whole string of parables to communicate ideas about heaven. That Paul does this speaks to the importance of the topic. Dwelling on these metaphors can help us understand how we live as disciples and do the hard work of disciple making.

I have found two different questions helpful in unwrapping these metaphors. First, we may look for similar ideas present in all three metaphors; we can learn from what they have in *common,* which may be the most important ideas. At the same time, each metaphor may also contribute a different unique understanding of the attitudes or principles of disciple making, and thus we can also look for and learn from what is *particular* to or different about each. We will do both. The following observations are by no means an exhaustive list. The nature of metaphors, like parables, is that they invite our repeated consideration. Indeed, I am reminded of what Eugene Peterson writes about parables in his wonderful book *Tell It Slant:*

Three Metaphors for Disciple Making

The parable is a form of speech that has a style all its own. It is a way of saying something that requires the imaginative participation of the listener. Inconspicuously, even surreptitiously, a parable *involves* the hearer. The brief, commonplace, unpretentious story is thrown into a conversation and lands at our feet, compelling notice. . . . And then we begin seeing connections. . . . Before we know it, we are involved . . .

Most parables have another significant feature. The subject matter is usually without apparent religious significance. They are stories about farmers and judges and victims, about coins and sheep and prodigal sons, about wedding banquets, building barns and towers and going to war, a friend who wakes you up in the middle of the night to ask for a loaf of bread, the courtesies of hospitality, crooks and beggars, fig trees and manure.

Spiritual masters are particularly fond of parables, for there is nothing more common than for people who want to talk about God to lose interest in the people they are talking to. Religious talk is depersonalized into godtalk. Godtalk is used to organize people in causes that no longer involve us, to carry out commands that no longer command us . . . Just then, the master drops a parable into the conversation. We stumble over it, no longer able to cruise along in the familiar word ruts. The parable forces attention, participation, involvement.[2]

Paul has not lost interest in Timothy. Paul is also a spiritual master. His metaphors of soldier, athlete, and farmer function as short, potent parables in much the way Peterson describes above. They are commonplace and unpretentious examples from everyday life, on their own devoid of explicit "religious significance." Yet they help us see connections. They involve us. If disciple making has digressed to mere *godtalk* in your experience, then let these metaphors grab your attention, participation, and involvement.

Life of Discipline

Ruth Haley Barton, in her book *Strengthening the Soul of your Leadership*, notes, "There is the tension between the need for an easy discipleship process through which we can efficiently herd lots of people and the patient, plodding and ultimately mysterious nature of the spiritual transformation process."[3] Barton was writing of our discipleship process in general, but

2. Peterson, *Tell It Slant*, 19.
3. Barton, *Strengthening the Soul of Your Leadership*, 27.

this is certainly true of the disciple making aspect of discipleship to Christ. There is no way to turn disciple making into an easy and efficient methodology as though it were an engineering problem. As noted, disciple making mustn't be a means of herding people. It requires patience and plodding. It also requires our own transformation—a point we will return to in the next chapter.

Paul recognized this. One aspect common to all three of Paul's metaphors immediately jumps out at me. Maybe it did for you also. The soldier, the athlete, and the farmer all must live a life of discipline, or what we might often refer to as self-discipline.[4] *Hardship* is another word the comes to mind to describe the sort of discipline involved in these three lifestyles. In *A Long Obedience in the Same Direction,* Eugene Peterson writes of one of the distorting—and harmful—lenses of our present-day culture.

> One aspect of *world* that I have been able to identify as harmful to Christians is the assumption that anything worthwhile can be acquired at once. We assume that if something can be done at all, it can be done quickly and efficiently. Our attention spans have been conditioned by thirty-second commercials. Our sense of reality has been flattened by thirty-page abridgements.
>
> It is not difficult in such a world to get a person interested in the message of the gospel; it is terrifically difficult to sustain the interest. Millions of people in our culture make decisions for Christ, but there is a dreadful attrition rate. Many claim to have been born again, but the evidence for mature Christian discipleship is slim.[5]

It is as though instead of the Great Commission of making disciples who obey, we have made only converts who want an insurance policy—and only short-term converts at that. What is lacking in Christian discipleship might

---

4. The word *discipline* has multiple meanings. I do *not* use the term in this chapter with the meaning of "punishment," but rather in the sense of "training": this sort of discipline might best be described as a willingness to work at something even when the work is difficult or unpleasant, or to make a decision to do (or not do) something keeping in mind a long-term good rather than a short-term pleasure (see Hebrews 11:25–26). It is an act of discipline to refuse that second helping of dessert or let the bowl of potato chips pass when partaking would be pleasurable but contrary to one's nutrition goals. The term *self-discipline* might help distinguish between this intended definition of discipline and the idea of punishment. As we will see in the next chapter, however, even "self-discipline" is not really what we need; we need our discipline to be empowered by something other than self. As Paul exhorts Timothy in 2 Timothy 2:1, we need to be "strong in the grace that is in Christ Jesus."

5. Peterson, *A Long Obedience in the Same Direction,* 15–16.

Three Metaphors for Disciple Making

be described as discipline: the long obedience in the same direction that Peterson gets at in the title of his book.

Consider the soldier, and in particular consider the Roman soldier of Paul's day. In addition to the training required before battle, being a Roman soldier also often involved a long grueling process of travel just to get to battle. Travel was not by military transport jet. It could take weeks or even months of marching across a countryside in all sorts of weather over all sorts of terrain just to reach the battlefield. I wonder if Paul, when he wrote "Join with me in suffering, like a good soldier of Christ Jesus," had in mind the suffering involved in this life of military discipline as much or more than the suffering that might result from injuries in the battle itself.

Of course a battle also requires discipline of a different sort: a complete concentration and single-minded focus on the task at hand. Without it, the soldier quickly becomes a casualty. Thus Paul reminds his readers that a soldier must not be entangled in everyday civilian life. Forgetting the demands of battle, and getting distracted by civilian affairs—whether during training or in battle—can be deadly. The soldier's life must be one of discipline. John Stott quotes Tertullian, a Roman writer and Christian apologist of the late second and early third centuries. By virtue of the time and culture he lived in, Tertullian could be expected to have a clearer understanding of what a Roman soldier was like than any twenty-first-century reader. He writes, "No soldier comes to the war surrounded by luxuries, nor goes into action from a comfortable bedroom, but from a makeshift and narrow tent, where every kind of hardship and severity and unpleasantness is to be found."[6] Paul's use of the soldier metaphor should go a long way to dispelling the false prosperity gospel that promises financial success and freedom from physical suffering ("health and wealth") to any Christian who displays enough faith—a so-called "faith" that the peddlers of this false gospel say is best displayed by given money to them. As Stott notes following his reference to Tertullian's quote, "Similarly, the Christian should not expect an easy time. If he is loyal to the gospel, he is sure to experience opposition and ridicule. He must 'share in suffering' with his comrades-in-arms."[7] This is certainly true of the Christian committed to disciple making.[8]

---

6. Tertullian, *Address to Martyrs,* chapter 2, para. 3. Alfred Plummer's translation, cited in Stott, *The Message of 2 Timothy,* 53.

7. Stott, *The Message of 2 Timothy,* 53

8. If Paul's teaching on suffering isn't enough to convince readers that the so-called

So too the life of the athlete. What pops into mind when I think of athletes is the large number of hours spent in training for every minute of actual competition. How many miles does a runner run alone in training before racing in the Olympics? How many practice javelin or hammer throws before the throw that counts? Most of the work of the athlete takes place out of the spotlight and without the cameras ready for instant replay—or as Paul may have noted in his day, outside the Coliseum and away from its crowds. I know many would-be athletes with athletic potential for whom competition is fun but for whom training is drudgery. Many drop out of serious athletics for that very reason. The athletes I know who have proven successful over the long term find training to be enjoyable at least some of the time. Even when it is not, they persist at it. And even when it is, it's still work and still requires discipline.

Of course hard work is no guarantee an athlete will win the prize. Many elite and hard-working athletes end a season having failed to capture the trophy. Some compete through an entire career without ever taking home the gold medal, or hoisting the Lombardi trophy that goes to the winner of the Super Bowl. But though discipline and hard work are no guarantee of athletic success, they are the path toward success. Put another way, while discipline will not guarantee that you win a trophy, lack of discipline is a pretty good guarantee that you will not win the trophy.

Then there is the farmer. A farmer characterizes discipline perhaps more than any other profession I can think of. (Maybe that's why I love Hannah's character in *Silverado* so much.) Several members of my church were dairy farmers at once point in their lives. I can remember small-group prayer breakfasts years ago with John, a friend who was working on a family dairy farm at the time. I and a couple other attendees would drag ourselves out of bed to get to the diner sleepy eyed at 7:30 AM. John would arrive having already been up working for three and a half hours, putting in more physical labor before I got my first cup of coffee than I would accomplish in a week. The athlete at least gets to compete in front of a cheering crowd every now and then after the grueling hours of practice and training. A soldier may not look forward to battle with all its dangers and risks, but a battle at least offers the opportunity for glory. Not so the work of farming.

---

prosperity gospel is false, we could also consider what he writes about the fruit of the Spirit; Paul tells us that this fruit is "love, joy, peace, forbearance, goodness, faithfulness, gentleness and self-control" (Galatians 5:22, NIV). Nowhere are we told that the fruit is physical health or material wealth. The discussion of the fruit of the spirit relates to our transformation, a topic we will return to in the next chapter.

Three Metaphors for Disciple Making

"However poor the soil, inclement the weather, or disinclined the farmer, he must keep at his work," Stott points out. "Having put his hand to the plough, he must not look back."[9]

In the opening paragraph of *A Long Obedience,* Peterson notes, "A person who makes a commitment to Jesus Christ as Lord and Savior does not find a crowd immediately forming to applaud the decision or old friends spontaneously gathering around to offer congratulations and counsel."[10] And I could add to that: the person who *continues* to live out that commitment to Christ in the subsequent days, weeks, months, years, and even decades, and who follows in a life of discipline, discipleship, and disciple making, also cannot expect a cheering crowd to greet her when she takes that extra time in the morning to read the Bible and pray, and root herself more deeply in the word as the foundation for her discipleship. Nor when she gets up on a Sunday morning and overcomes the inertia in order to meet her fellow believers for gathered worship as part of a body and family (even though she might not like all of the music). Nor when she keeps the appointment with the person she is mentoring, who may or may not show up this week. No more than the farmer can expect to step out the door of the farmhouse an hour or more before dawn and expect cheering and adoring crowds lined along the path to the barn waiving pom-poms and shouting with excitement, "Milk those cows. Milk those cows. Go. Rah!"

The metaphors are apt then. They prepare us for the mind-set we must have to live out the life of discipleship and disciple making, with that long obedience.

The Reward

Fortunately, hard work is not the only aspect the three metaphors have in common. All three vocations involve some sort of reward. With two of the three metaphors, the athlete and the farmer, Paul explicitly brings that reward to Timothy's attention as a highlight and reminder of the great hope that they share. With the metaphor of the soldier, it is at least implied.

The successful athlete, Paul reminds Timothy, works toward a goal of receiving a victor's crown. That the victor's crown in Paul's day would have been an evergreen wreath and not gold, silver, or bronze doesn't diminish its significance. That symbol of victory is the reward, the goal of every

---

9. Stott, *The Message of 2 Timothy,* 56.
10. Peterson, *A Long Obedience,* 15.

competing athlete. And it is a non-trivial one. Spectator events played an important role in the Roman empire. Olympic games, for example, dated back to ancient Greece approximately eight centuries before the time of Paul's letter, and continued under Roman rule. Athletes were viewed as heroes. Which is to say, not much has changed.

Even today, when a monetary award comes to the winner in addition to the trophy, for many athletes it is the glory of winning and holding the trophy—or wearing the victor's crown—that is the most meaningful and motivating prize. Most professional athletes will say they have one thing only as their goal at the start of each season: winning the league championship: the World Series, or the Super Bowl, or the Stanley Cup, or the NBA Finals, or the World Cup. Images of the adoration poured on members of the New England Patriots as they paraded around Boston in duck boats two days after winning the Super Bowl—and two weeks before I wrote this chapter—give evidence of the importance of those athletic victories. So do the invitations that come from the White House to winning teams. The frenzy around the World Cup in most South American, European, and African nations is even greater than the frenzy around any one particular sport in the United States. The victor gets a crown.

The farmer also receives a reward. It is not a wreath (or crown) to place on his head, but something rather more practical (though less glorious): the farmer receives a share of the crops. The reward to the farmer for their discipline and hard work is food on the table. That is to say, the reward is life itself. Metaphorically speaking, therefore, the farmer's reward may have the most in common with the reward Paul looked forward to, which he mentions near the end of his letter by returning to the sports metaphor: "I have fought the good fight, I have finished the race, I have kept the faith. Now there is in store for me the crown of righteousness, which the Lord, the righteous Judge, will award to me on that day—and not only to me, but also to all who have longed for his appearing" (2 Timothy 4:7–8, NIV).

The soldier also receives a reward for his discipline and hard work. One reason Paul might not mention it explicitly may be that the reward would have been so obvious to any of his readers. The soldier receives pay. More specifically, a soldier fighting in battle gets a portion of the spoils of war. That's the reward for victory. The punishment for defeat is often death. The contrast is sharp, then, and so then is motivation.

And this leads to a final comment on this section. There is a misconception that followers of Christ should not be concerned with a reward. It

Three Metaphors for Disciple Making

is true that Christians should not be looking for an *earthly* reward. That truth has run throughout this whole book, including the start of this chapter. Yet the promise of an eternal reward is central to the gospel.[11] Indeed, the promise of a resurrected body is at the core of the Christian hope. As Paul notes in one of his letters to the Corinthian church, the resurrection of Jesus and the promised resurrection for Christ's followers and disciple makers are intimately connected. If one is a hoax, so is the other. And if that resurrection promise is false, then Christianity is a fundamentally false religion, a big lie, and a waste of time, and Christ's followers are pitiable fools.[12] Paul points out something similar in his letter to the Romans, where he also suggests that the resurrection gives hope even in the midst of the suffering of believers[13]—a suffering he writes about often, including in his letter to Timothy.

Yet despite all these promises of resurrection and a reward throughout the New Testament, I still have often heard people ask, *Isn't it selfish to follow Christ only for a reward?* In some sense, the answer is, indeed, yes. From an eternal perspective, following Christian certainly could be described as a selfish choice: selfish in the sense that it is best for us. God doesn't ask us to do something that is ultimately bad for us. From one eternal perspective, believers in Christ are not different from unbelievers; it is not that unbelievers make an unselfish choice to reject Christ, while believers make a selfless choice to follow him. The difference isn't unselfishness as opposed to selfishness, but rather a question of faith, and therefore also of eternal perspective. The one who doesn't have faith in Christ may feel the need to look after their own interests rather than trusting God's plan. By contrast, the one who puts her faith in Christ believes that ultimately Christ has the best plan, and that this plan is for our good—even our eternal good—and therefore (selfishly speaking, but speaking out of faith) it makes sense in our temporal lives to live unselfishly. The crown of righteousness awaits us: a share of the crops; the reward that goes to the victor who lives for the commanding officer. Put another way, the Christian should indeed live unselfishly through this temporal pre-resurrection life even when it means

---

11. It is also true that following Christ is about far more than an afterlife, or eternal reward: the joy of a relationship with God begins here and now. In some sense, for the follower of Christ, the promised eternal life has already began. Though we also await a resurrected body and Christ's return in power, at which point the eternal life we have in God will come to its fullness.

12. See 1 Corinthians 15, especially verses 12–19 and 32.

13. See Romans 8:18–25.

persecution or suffering, but should do so *by faith* because of the promise of Christ and the knowledge that eternally this obedience to Christ is actually best for us.

The Weather and the Rules

Readers who spend time meditating on these metaphors may find more in common between them than what I have mentioned above. But let's turn now to insights that come from observing what is unique about each metaphor rather than what they have in common.

What strikes me most about farmers is their dependency on something beyond their own work. Yes, the farmer must work hard, but hard work alone is no guarantee of success. A farmer is as dependent on the weather as he is on his own labor. If the rain does not come in season, or if too much rain comes, or if rain or sunshine come in the wrong season, the crops will not thrive; the awaited harvest toward which so much labor was invested may never come, or may come with far less fruitfulness than was intended. The farmer's very life depends on many things outside the farmer's control. Indeed, control itself is but an illusion.

Even more than the weather, the farmer is also dependent on the soil and on processes of life that are also out of the farmer's control. A farmer may till the soil, fertilize it, and plant the seed. A farmer cannot, however, make a seed sprout and grow just as a farmer cannot control when the rains come, or how much rain comes. Likewise, the Christian committed to disciple making is fully dependent on God. God is the one who bears fruit. Our hard work, in and of itself, can accomplish nothing. We are still called to work hard, of course. But we are called to do so in dependence on God. This requires great faith. We are not in control. Yet it can also be freeing to realize that God is responsible, and to let go of our illusions of control. In the disciple-making process, I cannot force the disciple of Christ to grow any more than I can make myself more holy by working hard at it. (More on this in the next chapter.)

If you have never done so, I recommend meditating for a time on this aspect of the life of the farmer. Then take a few minutes and recognize how illusory your own sense of being in control really is. Of course you should do this remembering how hard a farmer works.

As with the metaphor of farmer, meditating on the metaphor of athlete also provides invaluable insights. "Anyone who competes as an athlete,"

Three Metaphors for Disciple Making

Paul writes, "does not receive the victor's crown except by competing according to the rules." What are these rules that must govern competition? One insight in particular stands out to me, especially when I consider the first-century notion Paul likely would have had of an athlete as opposed to the twenty-first-century idea that pops first into my mind. When I think of the word *athlete* today—or if a sports metaphor is used in church—the image likely comes from one of the big professional team sports played in the United States: football, basketball, baseball, hockey, or soccer. The rules in these sports, especially football, are tremendously complex—so much so that professional players and coaches sometimes make serious mistakes because they don't know them all, or because even knowing them and trying to follow them, they fail. A player lining up a foot or two behind the line of scrimmage in the recent Super Bowl proved to be a significant play; some argued that it impacted the outcome of the game. If we understand Paul's metaphor in the light of these modern sports, "competing according to the rules" could easily lead to destructive legalism, where we think that Christianity is all about learning a bunch of rules about things we aren't allowed to do (or are required to do), and making sure we don't (or do) do those things. Certainly God has given us moral guidelines for living in obedience, but these principles bear little in common with the sort of detailed rules that govern modern sports. Legalism may be one of the most damaging threats to discipleship and disciple making.

I suspect Paul had something very different in mind when he spoke about "the rules": an idea that would have come from the track and the field competitions common to an Olympic athlete. Running a marathon, or even a few laps around a track, is not about learning a huge book of complex rules. The rules are relatively simple and the primary rule has simply to do with running in the right direction, which is to say, running on the course. You can be the fastest runner in the world, but if you don't run in the direction you are supposed to run then you will not win the race. A similar comment can be made about field events, such as the javelin throw. It isn't enough just to be able to throw the javelin really far; it must be thrown in the correct direction or it doesn't count.

If you are wondering whether this idea of "rules" from these examples of running and throwing—and not the rules of a sport like football—are really what Paul had in mind for his metaphor, remember that Paul returns to his athlete metaphor near the end of the letter when he once again speaks of the prize awaiting him: the "crown of righteousness" which the Lord will award to him after he finishes running a race. Paul also uses the metaphor of an athlete running a race in 1 Corinthians 9:24, and the author of Hebrews (believed by many to be Paul) also uses the metaphor in Hebrews 12:1 (with the added note about the required endurance).

Getting back to the disciple maker, then, the implications of this metaphor are powerful. We can work as hard as we want—running fast, throwing things far—but if our efforts are not focused in the right direction, if they are not directed toward Christ and by Christ, then our efforts are in vain. Like the runner or javelin thrower following the rules, so too the disciple maker must keep his or her efforts focused in the right direction. It is not enough to be fast and strong and work hard. The only way to do this is to be rooted in Christ and in the word. The work cannot be accomplished by self-directed labor, no matter how hard we work.

The Battle

My final observation from Paul's three metaphors brings us back to the soldier. The observation is somewhat indirect. It is not so much about the specifics of the soldier, but about the implications of Paul even using this metaphor. A soldier implies an army, which implies a war. Certainly a farmer faces challenges. And an athlete faces competition. But a soldier faces hostile opposition. That Paul would compare following Christ and doing the work of disciple making with being a soldier implies that those who follow Christ are in a war. It also implies that there is an enemy.

This reality of war, strife, and enmity is present throughout all of Scriptures, from the third chapter of Genesis to the end of Revelation. As God tells the serpent after the fall of Adam and Even in the garden:

> "And I will put enmity
> between you and the woman,
> and between your offspring and hers;
> he will crush your head,
> and you will strike his heel." (Genesis 3:15, NIV)

Although God promises that through the offspring of Eve, the serpent's head will ultimately be crushed and the battle won, the rest of the history of the descendants of Eve will nonetheless play out in the context of this war. We live on a battlefield, and will continue to do so until we reach the other bookend, and the events of the final three chapters of Revelation.

Three Metaphors for Disciple Making

So what does it mean that we are soldiers living in a war? One observation from Paul's letter to Timothy is the reminder that we have a commanding officer whom we should seek to obey and please. Our commanding offer is Christ Jesus, who is also our savior. God is not simply a great cosmic vending machine we go to in order to get what we want. He does not exist simply as a therapist to make us feel good, standing idly by until we call for help. We are soldiers of Christ Jesus; he is our commanding officer.

Just a couple of weeks before I wrote this chapter, my pastor was preaching on Joshua 5, and the visitor who comes to Joshua on the way to Jericho.

> 13 Now when Joshua was near Jericho, he looked up and saw a man standing in front of him with a drawn sword in his hand. Joshua went up to him and asked, "Are you for us or for our enemies?"
>
> 14 "Neither," he replied, "but as commander of the army of the LORD I have now come." Then Joshua fell facedown to the ground in reverence, and asked him, "What message does my Lord have for his servant?" (Joshua 5:13–14, NIV)

As Pastor Allen noted, the fact that Joshua falls on his face in worship—and that the man accepts that worship—is an indication that this visitor is divine and not just an angelic visitor. God alone is worthy of worship. In light of 2 Timothy 2:4, which refers to us as soldiers of Christ, that the visitor identifies himself as the commander of the Lord's armies is further indication it is Christ. In any case, this speaks directly to this idea that we are in a war and God is our commander. So often we go to God asking God to be on our side. This seems to be what Joshua is doing. As it turns out, that is the wrong question; the question is not whether Jesus is on our side to win our battles, but whether we are on his side. The appropriate response to that recognition is worship.

A related observation is that we are not free to live selfishly, seeking our own pleasure. We are called to obey, and even to join in suffering. Of course, God is also gracious, and calls us his children. He invites us to bring all our requests before him, as well as all our sorrows. But this passage suggests that these requests should be subsidiary to the humble obedience we bring to him as his soldiers.

As soon as I raise the metaphor of being soldiers of Christ Jesus living in a war zone, however, I have one serious concern for how such language can, and often is, misused within the church. So often when I hear that language, it is from Christians trying to point at enemies within the world;

it is from Christians seeing other humans around them as the enemy; it is Christians trying to wage war on culture, or on some political entity. To return to a topic from earlier chapters, some use the metaphor of soldiers in a war for the purpose of fear-mongering.

I said earlier that the reality of battle runs through the Bible from the third chapter to the third-from-last chapter. Nowhere is it stated more clearly than in Paul's letter to the Ephesians. In Ephesians 6:10–18, Paul also makes use of the soldier metaphor, and he states most clearly that we are fighting a war. Yet he also makes it most clear that our battle is not against other humans, but against spiritual forces. Humans are not our enemy. Not even humans who are part of a different political party. "For our struggle is not against flesh and blood, but against the rulers, against the authorities, against the powers of this dark world and against the spiritual forces of evil in the heavenly realms" (Ephesians 6:10–18, NIV).

To put this in the context of 2 Timothy and Paul's warnings to Timothy, and to repeat a point I have already touched on, the big concern for Timothy is not opposition to Christianity from the outside, and it isn't even persecution. In fact, Paul's admonition to Timothy tells us we should be willing to suffer, and not that we should be fighting battles against other humans whom we believe might cause us to suffer. The real threat Paul warns of in 2 Timothy is false teaching, which comes from the evil one. It is a failure to make disciples. In fact, fear itself may be a bigger threat to the church than the object of fear. Following Christ should transform our culture, but we aren't at war with our culture. Be a soldier ready to fight the war, but fight the right war with the right commanding officer. Our battle is against the evil one, the tempter, the accuser, the serpent. And this leads us to the final chapters of this book.

6

The Lust of the Eyes and Flesh

A Threefold Look at Temptation, Part I

> One of the things I know for sure is that those who are looking to us for spiritual sustenance need us first and foremost to be spiritual seekers ourselves. They need us to keep searching for the bread of life that feeds our own souls so that we can guide them to places of sustenance for *their* own souls. Then, rather than offering the cold stone of past devotionals, regurgitated apologetics or someone else's musings about the spiritual life, we will have bread to offer that is warm from the oven of our intimacy with God.[1]
>
> —Ruth Haley Barton

IN MY ADULTHOOD, KNOWING something about skin cancer and the damage caused by ultraviolet radiation, I try to avoid spending too much time in direct sunlight without protection. I love being outdoors, but when I'm outside in direct sunlight I make a point of wearing a hat and sunscreen to protect my skin in addition to the Costa sunglasses that protect my eyes. For summer days on the water in very bright sunlight or thin mountain

---

1. Barton, *Strengthening the Soul of Your Leadership*, 29.

air, I have a pair of cool, lightweight, but high-SPF, fingertip-less fishing gloves as well as various bandanas or Buffs to put around my neck—and in extreme sunshine, even over my nose and cheeks and ears.

Not so when I was in high school. I used to like to get a tan. It was a status symbol of sorts. But here is the thing: I couldn't make my skin tan. None of us can. If I wanted an exercise in futility, I could sit inside in my room all day grunting and groaning like I was lifting weights at the gym, trying to force my pale skin to darken. Nothing would happen. No amount of self-effort can give me a tan.

The summer tan I desired could only come about as the result of the work of the sun and its rays. Though I couldn't make my skin get any darker through self-effort, I could head to the beach and place myself under the power of the sun and let that sunshine do its work of transforming my skin. I could put myself in a place to be tanned and transformed.

Disciples of Christ are called to the work of disciple making in the lives of others. We are called to be a part of God's transforming work—that is, to be transforming influences. For that to happen, however, we must also be open to God's transforming work in our own lives. As Ruth Haley Barton noted in the epigraph above, "One of the things I know for sure is that those who are looking to us for spiritual sustenance need us first and foremost to be spiritual seekers ourselves."

One helpful way to think about this (though by no means the only one) is in the context of obedience. Disciple making is about training in discipleship. Discipleship involves obedience. Remember where we began this book: with the Great Commission of Jesus to make disciples, teaching them to *obey*. The transformation process at work in our lives is one that brings us more fully into obedience to Christ through faith in Christ and relationship with Christ

Sin, by contrast, might be understood as the opposite of obedience; it is a word we use for *dis*obedience. Sin is the cause of our broken relationship with God. It is appropriate, therefore, for a book about disciple making to considers sin and disobedience. Those seeking to follow Christ must take the topic seriously. Though reading two chapters about sin may seem like a big downer, these chapters are actually full of hope.

To consider sin, we must also consider the enemy against whom we wage battle. Satan's goal is to destroy our relationship with God. Sin accomplishes that. Sin results in death, which spiritually speaking is separation from God. Satan works as a deceiver and tempter, as well as an accuser and

The Lust of the Eyes and Flesh

devourer. The goal of his deceit and temptation is to lead us into sin. The Bible suggests a threefold pattern to how Satan seeks to tempt us: three primary categories of temptation—aspects of human nature—that the enemy repeatedly uses or seeks to exploit. John, in his first epistle, describes that pattern as follows: "For everything in the world—the lust of the flesh, the lust of the eyes, and the pride of life—comes not from the Father but from the world" (1 John 2:16, NIV). I would describe these three types of desires as follows: 1. a desire to *possess*, 2. A desire for physical *pleasure*, and 3. a desire for *power*: a desire to be in control, to have authority, to be god.

Interestingly, the same threefold pattern of temptation can also be seen in the tempting of Eve (and Adam) in the garden of Eden by the serpent, who is later (Revelation 12:9) associated with Satan. "When the woman saw that the fruit of the tree was good for food and pleasing to the eye, and also desirable for gaining wisdom, she took some and ate it" (Genesis 3:6a, NIV). Eve was led to believe that the fruit would bring her physical pleasure (it was "good to eat"); it appealed to her desire to possess and to the "lust of the eyes" (it was "pleasing to the eye"); and lastly the serpent tells her it would make her more like God, more in control. Interestingly enough, thousands of years later in the first-century church, John had to warn about the same three things. And, I would add, two thousand years after that, those three sorts of temptations are still present in the lives of believers; Satan has not had to be very creative in tempting us.

Similarly, the tempting of Jesus after his forty-day fast in the desert also follows a threefold pattern. Satan again appears as tempter. First he tempts Jesus to turn stone into bread in order to meet a physical desire. He then appeals to the lust of the eyes and the desire to possess, offering Jesus all the wealth of the earth. Finally, he taunts Jesus to prove that he is God, and to exhibit his power and control, by commanding angels to come and rescue him. Of course where Adam and Eve failed to resist temptation, Jesus succeeded. Still, three different times in Scriptures—in Genesis, in the Gospels, and in one of the final New Testament epistles—we see this threefold description of temptation, appealing to a desire to possess, a physical desire, and a desire for power. There are other meaningful ways we might categorize these three temptations, and certainly there is overlap between them, but I think this understanding can be helpful in our struggle against sin.

How can it be helpful? I believe God has given us strength and tools for our struggle—or weapons, to use one of Paul's metaphors. I am not suggesting some simple three-step program to eliminate sin from our lives. That won't happen in this age. Though Christ on the cross defeated death which is the ultimate consequence of sin, the final victory and the end of sin in this world won't be realized until Christ returns. But we can ask how to win the *next* battle. In this chapter and the next we look at this threefold temptation seen in Genesis, in Jesus in the desert, and in 1 John, seeking principles and models for our struggle against sin.

First, however, we must look at some important biblical principles in contrast to common misguided ways to think about sin.

The Struggle: Wrong Approaches to Sin and Temptation

There are three popular but misguided ways to think about sin. (Indeed, there are many wrong ways to think about it, but three in particular we consider in this chapter.) The first wrong idea is that we can conquer sin and temptation in our lives by striving really hard against it. *If I just work really hard*, we deceive ourselves, *I can overcome this sin in my life.*

You can't. Period. Self-effort at defeating sin in our lives will be no more successful than self-effort at trying to accomplish our own salvation. Self-effort at defeating sin would be no more successful than me lying in bed trying to make my skin tan. We are saved by God's grace, and only by his grace, at work through Jesus on the cross. The entire New Testament makes that abundantly clear. Paul's letter to the Ephesians contains one of the clearest and also best-known expressions of this principle. "For it is by grace you have been saved, through faith—and this is not from yourselves, it is the gift of God—not by works, so that no one can boast" (Ephesians 2:8–9, NIV). Likewise, the process of our sanctification—our being made holy, and freed from sin's power—is also accomplished only by God's grace through the work of his Holy Spirit in our lives. In the seventh chapter of his letter to the Roman church, Paul captures a common experience for those who have struggled, and inevitably failed, to overcome sin by our own self effort. Thus he does not say to Timothy, *depend on your own strength and ability*; instead, at the start of the passage that has been central to this book, he writes, "Be strong *in the grace that is in Christ Jesus*," (2 Timothy 2:1a, NIV, emphasis added). If you want a tan, let the power of the sun work on you.

The Lust of the Eyes and Flesh

This, not surprisingly, leads to a second common misguided way to think about our battle against sin: the false idea that since all human struggle against sin will fail, we ought not struggle at all. Though this approach could lead to a life full of obvious outward sins, in some ways it may be a less dangerous temptation than the first one. Pride is the biggest hindrance to a walk with God. We are better off knowing we can't defeat sin by ourselves than filling ourselves with pride in thinking we can. Nonetheless, choosing not to struggle against sin is also a wrong approach. The author of Hebrews chastised his audience toward the end of his letter, noting: "In your struggle against sin, you have not yet resisted to the point of shedding your blood" (Hebrews 12:4, NIV). The author's assumption is that his audience *should* be struggling against sin, and his criticism isn't that they are struggling too hard, but that they are not struggling enough. I wrote earlier that sin is disobedience to God. That's a mild word. Sin is rebellion against God. It is war against God. Sin leads to death. Sin *is* death. It is destructive in our lives. It is destructive in the world. Our struggle against sin—our resistance, the author suggests—should be of such intensity that we are willing to shed blood.

We must resist sin. We must struggle against it. We must also do so knowing that if such a struggle is relying upon our own strength, then the struggle will fail. So how do we struggle? We're coming to that. But first, one last wrong and destructive idea about sin that relates to the first.

Sin, in some misconceptions, is defined by a list of things we aren't supposed to do. Sin is defined in the negative: *don't do this, it is sin; don't do that either, it also is sin; and definitely don't do that, which is a really bad sin.*

Certainly there are destructive behaviors God has called us to avoid: temptations we are told to resist or flee from. We must not murder or steal or lie. We must not commit adultery. We must not worship idols or take the Lord's name in vain. There are a few others we could also add. We shouldn't mistreat strangers, or withhold the wages of workers, or oppress the poor. Overall, however, the biblical list of prohibitions is surprisingly short. In any case, this false view—the idea that sin is defined as a list of bad things— is an aspect of legalism, which is one of the most destructive attitudes or approaches we can have toward sin. Like the previous two topics, this has been dealt with in many thoughtful books and essays. Nonetheless, let us briefly consider (in the context of the previous chapters of this book) two ways this type of legalism can be destructive.

The first problem with this view is that we are tempted to make a list of things to avoid, and then somehow convince ourselves that if we can avoid those things we are free from sin. In doing so, we typically create a list of *outward* sins. Even more specifically, we make a list of sins we see other people doing, but which we are (outwardly) free of, thus making the contrast between (those) sinners and (us) non-sinners more obvious. For example, as long as I'm not required to consider the attitude of my heart and things like pride or selfishness, I could make a decently long list of "sins" I can mostly avoid because they aren't strong temptations for me. I've never murdered somebody, and I think it's likely I never will. (Don't ask me if I've thought harmful thoughts toward anybody, though.) I don't have a problem with substance abuse. (Unless you count coffee, or a lack of discipline around chocolate or ice cream.) I've been married to my first wife for more than thirty years, most of which has been quite joyful, and I've never had an adulterous affair. I don't even feel tempted to have an affair. (I'd rather not talk about my lustful *thoughts*, however.) One possible result of this thinking is pride and self-righteousness, if we somehow deceive ourselves into thinking we have defeated sin because we have avoided the things on the list. And with self-righteousness comes a sense of condemnation or judgment of others.

Another frequent result of this false thinking is that we live fake lives, lacking vulnerability or integrity, showing a surface veneer of law-keeping while hiding (especially from our Christian brothers and sisters) the sinfulness of our hearts that we can't help but be aware of ourselves. As a result, we never get the help we need in our struggles against sin, and are also unable to offer the help to others in their struggles.

Viewing sin as a list of "do-nots" also fails to recognize that sin is just as often not doing something God has called us to do as it is doing something he commanded us not to do. Jonah may not have murdered, stolen, lied, cheated, or fornicated when he refused God's call to go to Nineveh, but he most certainly disobeyed and rebelled. And thus he missed the call of God. Obedience is trusting God's plan, and following it, because we know that plan is good (even if it may be difficult). Obedience is not merely avoiding a bunch of (possibly pleasurable) things that God has prohibited (perhaps because we view God as a cosmic spoilsport).

Earlier in the book I mentioned going to a big Christian missions conference during my freshman year of college. What I didn't describe was the biggest impact of that conference in my life. To say I was not the most popular kid in my high school would be an understatement. I started high school as the shortest male in my class. I was nerdy and bookish in addition to being uncoordinated and unathletic. I wasn't interested in being part of the partying culture, and I couldn't get into the sports culture. I was an outsider. One thing I was modestly good at, however, was downhill skiing. I wouldn't have been considered good by the standards of a mountain state like Maine, Vermont, Colorado, or Alaska, but for a rural Massachusetts kid I was fine—not because I was athletic, but simply because I'd grown up skiing and devoted a lot of time to it. When looking at colleges, I kept in mind proximity to skiing and to fishing, and chose a small college in rural New Hampshire that had its own ski area. Skiing was my escape from my unpopularity: the place I could feel good about myself. By junior and senior year of high school, I was one of the top couple of skiers on the high school team. My winter vacations were devoted to skiing, and though I was not in general a truant or a church-skipper, a day of skiing could lure me away from both school and church.

One of the main speakers at the conference I attended December of that first year of college was Rebecca Pippert, author of several books including *Out of the Salt Shaker and Into the World.* Pippert spoke about the type of idolatry common in the United States, and about how to identify our idols: the false gods we worshipped. Nearly forty years later, I remember her offering three questions to help us identify our idols:

1. Where do we spend our time?
2. Where do we spend our money?
3. Where do we get our significance?

It didn't take me long to realize that, for me, the answer to all three questions was skiing. I took jobs as a high school student just to earn money to pay for lift tickets, and during my senior year of high school I dropped quite a few dollars on some higher-end racing skis. I probably spent at least twenty full days a winter on the slopes, plus many afternoons and half-days. And when I say "full days", I mean that I would get to the slope half an hour before opening so I could be on the first chair up the mountain in the morning, and my goal was always to be one of the last skiers up at the end of the day before the ski patrol rode up and the lift closed. If the weather was really miserable, when I'd reach a flatter section of trail I'd spin around and ski backwards to keep wind and ice from lashing my face—but I'd never just quit and head into the lodge.

As for my sense of significance, it also came from skiing. *Kids at school may be unkind to me*, I thought, *but I'm a better skier than they are. On the slopes, I have worth.*

And with those thoughts came the conviction that I was supposed to give up skiing. I had little doubt God was speaking to me. I argued with him for a few weeks. The arguments went something like this, repeated over and over again several times a day:

Me: There is nothing inherently sinful about downhill skiing.

God: That's right. There isn't. But I want you to give it up.

Me: I spent a lot of time skiing with my older brother, and that is worthwhile time together, in relationship building and fellowship.

God: Your relationship with your brother is a good thing, and spending time with him is a good thing. But I want you to give up skiing.

Me: Skiing is a healthy way to get exercise and spend time outdoors enjoying the beauty of creation.

God: It sure can be. But I want you to give up skiing.

Eventually I conceded the argument. One thing that helped me out was that I had broken my arm just before Christmas, so during this entire argument I wasn't out on the slopes every day. Otherwise, it might have been too difficult to quit. Still, I made one last attempt to escape. None of the conversation with God above happened with words I could hear with my ears, nor was there anything in the Bible about downhill skiing. Was it possible that all of this was just in my own thoughts—just guilt feelings, and not really God speaking? I hoped so. Also, I was pretty sure that I wouldn't be able to give up skiing unless I fully committed to the decision and sold my skis. I was an addict. The temptation to ski would be too great, I thought. I had covered my dorm room walls with ski posters, and my skis sat prominently in my room by the door. So one day I knelt down by my bed in my dorm and I prayed a prayer something like this: *God, I'm willing to give up skiing if you want me to. But I need to be able to sell my skis, and I've spent a lot of money on them. If you want me to give up skiing, you need to enable me to sell my skis for a fair price.*

Finishing the prayer, I thought I was pretty safe. That last clause in the prayer felt like a good defense against actually having to go through with the decision.

The Lust of the Eyes and Flesh

Except about fifteen minutes later, a friend stopped by my room, and with him was another person I had never met: a friend of his from home who happened to be visiting campus for the weekend. That friend of a friend saw the skiing posters plastered across my walls and commented that he was interested in taking up skiing. I commented that I was selling my skis and giving up skiing—though the reason for my decision felt both too painful and too odd to explain, so I left it unsaid. Turns out this visitor was not only my height and weight, but had my exact same shoe sizes. My skis and poles were perfect for him, and he said my boots felt like they were made for him. Half an hour after I prayed that prayer, the stranger walked out of my room with all my ski equipment. I never saw it again. I got one check right then, and another a few weeks later. I pulled the posters off my wall, and that was it.

Skiing, in and of itself, is not a sin. For me to continue skiing, however, when God called me to give it up, would have been disobedient. It also would have shut me off in many ways from the transforming work God had started in my life: the transformation that would continue in the years to come. Obedience is not just about a list of sins to avoid. To seek transformation in my life while refusing to obey God's call would have been like seeking a suntan while staying in my room.

And this brings us back to the central point of all of this. Obedience, and thus discipleship, is ultimately about our transformation. It is about God's work in our lives to make us more like him. More like him does indeed mean less sinful, of course. But being like Christ is so much deeper and more joyful than merely living a life in which we avoid certain behaviors or activities. In another of his daily devotion series on Ephesians, Mark Roberts reflects on Ephesians 4:22–24:

> [R]enewal is God's ongoing work in us. We do not renew ourselves. God does it. This does not happen completely in the moment of salvation. Rather, the renewal that begins when we first receive God's grace in Christ continues throughout our lives. It is something in which we participate by opening ourselves to the Lord, being available for his renewing work, and following the lead of the Spirit. A variety of spiritual practices—such as prayer, devotional reading of Scripture, and corporate worship—help us to share with the Spirit in our being made new.[2]

---

2. Roberts, "Be Renewed in the Spirit of your Mind."

Note the important points made by Paul in Ephesians, and emphasized by Mark Roberts. We cannot defeat sin in our lives by our own human effort. As Roberts notes, that must be "God's ongoing work in us." In the words of Paul on which Roberts was commenting, you are "to be made new in the attitude of your minds" (Ephesians 4:23). This phrase is in the passive voice, meaning it is not something we do, but rather something done to us, or in us, or for us. It is God's work. And yet in the same passage, Paul also writes in the active voice, "put off your old self," implying we are involved in this work of renewal. "We participate," Roberts notes. The strength we must draw on in discipleship and disciple making, as Paul writes to Timothy, is not our strength but the Lord's. But in the same breath Paul still tells Timothy to be strong.

Yes, disciple making does involve obedience. Yet the work and the goal of discipleship and disciple making is transformation. It is our renewal. Obedience and freedom from sin is not the *means* to renewal; it is the *result* of God's work of renewal. We don't stop sinning and start obeying in order that we are renewed, but rather when we open ourselves up for renewal then obedience becomes the pattern of our lives as a result of that renewal. As Roberts noted in another devotion on the same passage, "Our lives in Christ are a long process of ongoing renewal through the Word and Spirit as we live in communion with the Triune God and God's people. In Ephesians 4:23, the present tense of 'to be made new' reminds us of this fact."[3]

The work of disciple making is the work of walking alongside others and helping open them up and equip them for this ongoing process of transformation and renewal. Note that this language is not my language nor is it the language of Mark Roberts; it is Paul's language. In a passage from Romans 12, just before the passage we cited earlier where he uses the metaphor of the body, Paul writes: "Do not conform to the pattern of this world, but be transformed by the renewing of your mind" (Romans 12:2, NIV). There it is: transformation and renewal. Transformation that comes through renewal. Which also involves being freed from the patterns of this world that would conform us. Since renewal involves our minds, we also need to consider what we feed most often into our minds—that is, if we desire God's word and not the world's pattern to be the most important influence. In any case, this is another reason why disciple making also requires our own discipleship to Christ, and our own ongoing transformation

---

3. Roberts, "You Are A Work in Progress."

and renewal: why the disciple maker is both a teacher and an example of Christ. Passing on knowledge is not enough. We pass on our lives.

In a Renovaré podcast interview with Nathan Foster, Rebecca Konyndyk DeYoung (author of *Glittering Vices* and *Vainglory*) contrasts a healthy goal of transformation into Christlike character with a misguided view that sin is simply a list of things not to do. "The pressing more question isn't, 'Am I permitted to do this thing? Is it the right thing to do?' The pressing moral question is, 'If I practice this, and pursue this regularly for the next ten years, what kind of person would I become? What kind of character would I develop?'"[4] The interview goes on to explore the importance of spiritual disciplines in this Spirit-driven process of transformation, which both ties back to Mark Roberts's reference above to the importance of the "variety of spiritual practices," and also leads us to our next section.

On Spiritual Disciplines

One work I have not yet mentioned, though it would have been relevant in every preceding chapter of this book, is Richard Foster's *Celebration of Discipline*. It is one of a handful of books I recommend to anyone desiring to be a disciple of Christ, and one I have read multiple times myself and used for numerous small group discussions. The book was transformative in my life and thinking. "The desperate need," Foster writes in the third sentence of his first paragraph, "is not for a greater number of intelligent people, or gifted people, but for deep people."[5] Which is to say, the need is for a greater number of committed disciples, who (to reference Eugene Peterson's titular phrase) pursue the long obedience in the same direction. I'm not surprised that many of the deep people I know have also been influenced by Foster's work. With its publication in 1978, Richard Foster brought to light for many Christians the importance of spiritual discipline and of the spiritual disciplines.

Perhaps as a result of that book, many other important works have since followed bringing new insights, and helping a new generation of believers understand and benefit from the practices I first discovered in Foster's book. These include many works by Dallas Willard such as *Spirit of the Disciplines*. During the months I was writing this book, my wife and I co-led a Bible study using another approach to understanding spiritual

4. DeYoung, "Deadly Sins and Their Remedies."
5. Foster, *Celebration of Discipline*, 1.

disciplines: a series of guides written by Jan Johnson collectively titled *Spiritual Disciplines: Bible Studies and Practices to Transform Your Soul*. The nonprofit Renovaré organization (renovare.org) is also devoted to spiritual renewal, and offers tremendous resources including retreats and conferences, podcasts, and other print and online materials with a special interest in spiritual disciplines as a means toward renewal.

As with the topic of sin, it is important to recognize some misconceptions in thinking around spiritual disciplines even as we highlight the importance. There are several misconceptions, and this short section will barely do justice to the topic. Foster mentions some in his introduction, and all three books mentioned above will help along these lines, along with the material from Renovaré. For now I will just mention two important points that relate to this chapter.

First, practicing spiritual disciplines will *not* make God love us more. They will not earn us points in heaven. God does not keep a tally of how many times you fast or meditate or take a retreat of silence so that he can offer you an extra reward, either now or when Christ returns. One of the lies I already mentioned is the destructive prosperity gospel that preaches that following God is a means toward material rewards on earth: health and wealth. God's blessings *may* include material blessings at some times for some people. Yet a life of faith will also at times lead to suffering and hardship. So, too, the spiritual disciplines are not a means to extract some sort of reward from God any more than making a monetary contribution "of faith" to some organization is a means to a reward from God. Those are false and destructive teachings. A related point is that the disciplines aren't just for special spiritual people. As Foster notes, "God intends the Disciplines of the spiritual life to be for ordinary human beings: people who have jobs, who care for children, who must wash dishes and mow lawns."[6]

Another false idea is that if we work really hard at spiritual disciplines we will become more holy. This idea may sound more spiritual than the deceit of the previous paragraph, but it is every bit as damaging. If practicing spiritual disciplines is just part of self-directed effort, it will fail. This is really just another way of pointing out what I noted in the previous section: that human effort will not overcome sin. Indeed, our inability to defeat sin by our own strength is precisely why we need the disciplines.

Having acknowledged that, the practice of spiritual disciplines are tremendously helpful. As Mark Roberts wrote in the passage quoted in the

---

6. Foster, *Celebration of Discipline*, 1.

The Lust of the Eyes and Flesh

previous section, they "help us to share with the Spirit in our being made new." While spiritual disciplines won't succeed as a self-effort to make us holy, they do open us up to God's work. A good analogy is the preparations of Advent for the coming Messiah: readying our hearts, and making level paths. We can't make the Messiah come, nor can we do the work of the Messiah. The work of the Messiah is the work of the Messiah. And the work of the Holy Spirit is the work of the Holy Spirit. But we *are* all called to prepare the way: to ready ourselves for the work that is ultimately God's. Again, to use my own metaphor, we can't will our skin to tan (and given the dangers of skin cancer we probably shouldn't try) but we can place ourselves in the transforming power of sunlight. Spiritual disciplines can work in that way. Richard Foster writes, "When we despair of gaining inner transformation through human power of will and determination, we are open to a wonderful new realization: inner righteousness is a gift from God to be graciously received. The needed change is God's work, not ours. The demand is for an inside job, and only God can work from the inside." He goes on a few paragraphs later to elaborate, making a point about disciplines relating directly to our struggle against sin. "We do not need to be hung on the horns of the dilemma of either human works or idleness. God has given us the Disciplines of the spiritual life as a means of receiving his grace. The Disciplines allow us to place ourselves before God so that he can transform us."[7]

Jan Johnson gets at the same idea in her book on spiritual disciplines. She begins with a question, "Have you ever wondered how God changes people?" The very phrasing of this question already implies (correctly) that it is God who changes people and not we who change ourselves. She explains in the next paragraph. "God desires to transform our souls. This transformation occurs as we recognize that God created us to live in an interactive relationship with the Trinity. Our task is not to transform ourselves, but to stay connected with God in as much of life as possible.... We connect with God through spiritual disciplines."[8]

A second important benefit of spiritual disciplines such as fasting or silence is that the practice may help point out the root of some of our temptations. DeYoung, in the same Renovaré podcast interview with Nathan Foster, also speaks of how the practice of disciplines won't succeed as means of making us better by self-effort. However they can help expose not

---

7. Foster, *Celebration of Discipline*, 5–6.
8. Johnson, *Spiritual Disciplines Companion*, 7–8.

only the areas of our sin but also the root causes of the temptation. This sort of revelation can help us turn those areas over more fully to God. She concludes this beautifully, noting, "The practice of the disciples is to put your health in the hands of the great physician."[9]

And now we can turn to the lust of the flesh, the lust of the eyes, and the boastful pride of life.

The Lust of the Flesh and the Lust of the Eyes

Of the threefold temptations we see in the story of the fall, in the account of Jesus in the wilderness, and in John's epistle, the type of sin that often comes first to mind for many believers is the lust of the flesh. Because these sins by nature involve the body, they are outward in form and easier to spot, and thus also often easiest to judge (usually in others). The lust of the eyes is a close second. There are enough similarities between these two lusts that we can address them both together.

In less biblical language, the "lust of the flesh" might be translated simply as the desire for physical pleasure. We might think, for example, of sexual sins like adultery. I have often observed within churches a certain view—implicit if not explicit—that these "sins of the flesh" are the worst type of sins. A significant amount of attention is often given to them. And there is no doubt that sexual sins, especially adultery, can be very damaging. So too can gluttony or drunkenness.

Before looking at how we may draw on God's strength and grace in dealing with sins of the flesh, let us consider more carefully the nature of these sins. As a starting point, keep in mind that physical pleasure in and of itself is not bad. In fact, quite the opposite: it is a gift from God. God made our bodies. We are not intended to be *merely* spiritual beings, ascetically eschewing bodily experience or pleasure. As bodily beings created in the image of God, we were made capable of experiencing physical or material pleasure. How great is that! Strawberries and blueberries (with cream), chocolate, backrubs, and also the physical pleasure of sexual intimacy are all part of what God created us capable of experiencing as part of our physical existence in a physical universe that God repeatedly proclaimed "good" and "very good" (Genesis 1).

In his book *Mere Christianity*, C. S. Lewis writes, "There is no good trying to be a purely spiritual creature. That is why [God] uses material

9. DeYoung, "Deadly Sins and Their Remedies".

The Lust of the Eyes and Flesh

things like bread and wine to put the new life into us. We may think this rather crude and unspiritual. God does not: He invented eating. He likes matter. He invented it."[10] In his book *The Narnian*, Alan Jacobs notes the following about Lewis's fiction: "Perhaps the greatest resource on which he draws—and it is a mighty one—is, simply, *delight*. He calls us to take note of what gives us pleasure, for though our pleasures can indeed lead us astray, they are in their proper form great gifts from God."[11] The late Mark Heard, one of my favorite songwriters, used the phrase *pious anhedonia*[12] in his song "Straw Men" to critique the false teaching that bodily pleasure is somehow inherently sinful, and that an inability to feel pleasure (*anhedonia*) would actually be a sign of piousness or spiritual maturity; the character in the song judges the masses for dancing, while he himself is unable to appreciate beauty or gender.

Of course some of the greatest gifts God has given are also often most under attack. Sexual intimacy in the context of marriage is a good and wondrous thing. The pursuit of sexual pleasure outside of the commitment of marriage is degrading and destructive.

Simply enjoying pleasure, however, is not the root of the temptation that John refers to as the "lust of the flesh." The temptation—what turns our experience of pleasure into something sinful—is when we love pleasure *more* than we love God. This is what Paul warns Timothy about in 2 Timothy 3:4. It is what Jesus warns of in his parable in Luke 8:14: not that pleasure is evil, but that riches and pleasure may become like thorns that "choke" out our spiritual life. When we love pleasure more than we love God, then we pursue pleasure even when it means disobedience to God. When our pursuit of pleasure causes us to disobey, then the pursuit is wrong; a root of that sin is loving pleasure more than God.[13] Pursuing pleasure as our ultimate goal is destructive. By contrast, accepting with gratitude the pleasures God grants us by his grace is actually a means of delighting in God, and as such is an act of worship.

And here is where Satan as tempter is also a deceiver. Physical pleasures, though not fundamentally bad in and of themselves, will not ultimately

---

10. Lewis, *Mere Christianity*, Section II.5.
11. Jacobs, *The Narnian*, 189.
12. The song is titled "Straw Men" and was recorded on the album *Ashes and Light*. When I first heard the song, I had to look up the word *anhedonia* in a dictionary.
13. We could also argue that, at the root of pleasure-loving, is pride, fear, or a lack of faith. We will explore this more in the following sections.

fulfill us. Pleasures are—well, they are pleasurable. But that pleasure is fleeting. Rebecca DeYoung also summarizes a point made by Augustine. Noting the danger of "pursuing a finite created good with a passion that will only be satisfied by an infinite creator," she concludes, "You can't fill the longing you are created for with these finite things."[14]

Paul David Tripp gets at similar ideas, but with reference to our awe, and the need to be in awe of God and not of ourselves or things of this world.

> *Material things are for your pleasure.* Biblical faith doesn't curse the material world, and it is not antipleasure. God created a gloriously beautiful and pleasurable world. Consider the multihued sunset. Think about the gorgeous coat of a zebra. Listen to the melodious songs of the birds. Consider the vast array of colors, textures, and tastes of the food you eat. Imagine standing in front of a masterpiece painting or listening to a famous piece of music. Think of the beauty of the grain of wood or the swirling stripes that course their way through a piece of marble. Remember the pleasure of a kiss or the succulence of a ripe piece of fruit . . .
>
> You should never feel guilty for pursuing, participating in, and enjoying the pleasures of the material world God created. What you and I need to guard against is allowing awe of those pleasures to become the principle motivator of our hearts. When awe of material things rules your heart, then you will live for material things, and when you live for material things you will do just about anything to gain them, maintain them, keep them, and enjoy them. . . . Such a materialistic attitude is not only morally dangerous but is also a violation of the reason for which you and I were created. It is wrong for material cravings to dominate our hearts and lifestyles.[15]

Pleasure isn't bad, Tripp explicitly reminds us. Quite the contrary, it's a good gift; God created us to enjoy it, but in the proper context.

Note that without really trying, we've also already begun also to address the desire to possess, which I associate with the "lust of the eyes." In the same breath in which he mentions pleasures choking out the seed planted by the sower, Jesus also speaks of the choking power of our possessions. And certainly DeYoung's (and Augustine's) note about pursuing finite created goods applies equally to worldly possessions as it does to

---

14. DeYoung, "Deadly Sins and Their Remedies."
15. Tripp, *Awe*, 111–12.

The Lust of the Eyes and Flesh

physical pleasures. Oddly, the American church—perhaps gazing through a lens of Western consumerism and commercialism (and also Western materialism and capitalism), and deceived by the false teachings of the prosperity gospel—is often quite accepting of the desire to possess even while it harshly judges certain sins associated with pleasure. There is a strong biblical argument that God created us able to experience pleasure as a good gift, but some biblical indications that we actually are *not* created to possess things. In our modern secular setting in a fallen world, it seems that some possessions are a necessity in life—and are certainly not sinful in and of themselves any more than pleasure is. But while physical pleasure was a part of Eden before the fall, and would seem also to be a part of our new heavenly kingdom when Christ returns, personal possessions are not a part of either. Certainly the *pursuit* of possessions, or loving possessions more than we love God, is sinful and destructive. "No one can serve two masters," Jesus points out in his Sermon on the Mount. "Either you will hate the one and love the other, or you will be devoted to the one and despise the other. You cannot serve both God and money" (Matthew 6:24, NIV). The lust of the eyes and the lust of the flesh go hand in hand.

Back to the lie, then. Satan wants us to believe that pleasure and possessions will fulfill us and make us happy. In fact, the pursuit of them will make us numb to God. And here is where a biblical foundation is so important in discipleship and disciple making. Our best defense against lies is being firmly rooted in what is true. God has already empowered us to resist the work of the tempter and deceiver, however to receive that power we must deepen those roots and dwell on what is true. This is why our first foundational principle with which we began this book is that disciple making must be rooted in the transforming word of God.

One of the most important truths to dwell on is modeled most wonderfully by Moses, and was described by the author of Hebrews in characterizing why Moses was a hero of the faith. "By faith Moses, when he had grown up, refused to be known as the son of Pharaoh's daughter. He chose to be mistreated along with the people of God rather than to enjoy the fleeting pleasures of sin. He regarded disgrace for the sake of Christ as of greater value than the treasures of Egypt, because he was looking ahead to his reward" (Hebrews 11:24–26, NIV). The author acknowledges, as Moses also certainly knew, that certain types of sin may be pleasurable. That's one reason they are tempting. Even in circumstances when I ought not have it, good dark chocolate is a temptation for me. So are potato chips and ice cream. They are tempting because they bring me physical pleasure. Something in my taste buds sends chemical signals to my brain triggering pleasure sensors. As much as my wife loves them, however, I am not tempted to illicitly snitch Brussels sprouts.

What Moses understood, though, is that physical pleasure partaken of sinfully, and not as a gift from God enjoyed with gratitude, is "fleeting"; it doesn't last. Likewise, he also recognized that the "treasures of Egypt" that tempt the eye were also fleeting. Although Moses might have taken momentary pleasure giving in to either the lust of the eyes or the lust of the flesh, he understood that such pursuits would have hindered his taking part in God's plan for him, and would have blocked his delight in the much greater treasure that comes from following God.

This might be explained in philosophical terms. As God's image-bearers, we are beings of body, of mind, and of spirit. All three aspects of our humanness are both real and good, and our full humanness involves all three in full integration. This idea is rooted in a biblical worldview.[16] Moreover, we have terms for what *feels* good to each part of our triune personhood: that which feels good to the body, we call *pleasure*; that which feels good to the mind, we call *happiness;* that which feels good to the spirit, we call *joy*. In some sense, we were created to delight in all three: pleasure, happiness, and joy. All are good. It is important not to confuse them, however, even though some mistakenly use the terms *pleasure, happiness,* and *joy* interchangeably. Joy is the deepest of these three, and the only one that is eternal. At the most foundational level, we were created for joy. Happiness is fleeting. Anybody who has ever experienced a roller coaster of good news followed by bad knows this. Physical pleasure is more fleeting still. The moment the last bit of chocolate or ice cream is dissolved in my mouth, my taste buds are longing for more. And everybody knows how difficult it is to eat just one potato chip. For some in the world today, the desire for sexual pleasure seems insatiable. Why? Precisely because the physical pleasure it brings is fleeting; it does not satisfy in a lasting way, and thus must be frantically repeated.

---

16. Dick Keyes, in his book *Beyond Identity*, has a fascinating and important treatment of what defines or shapes our identity, contrasting the most fleeting with the most permanent and especially that which is eternal. This is another of the handful of books I recommend to anyone seeking to grow in faith as a disciple of Christ, and to walk with a biblical worldview. It relates closely to the concepts touched upon here of body, mind, and spirit, and corresponding states of pleasure, happiness, and joy. For a fuller treatment of this, see also my earlier book *The Mind and the Machine*.

The Lust of the Eyes and Flesh

Joy, a state of the spirit, is deep and lasting. And just as it is possible to feel happiness even when our bodies are not experiencing pleasure—think of an NFL football player who has just won a Super Bowl in part through sacrificing his body—so too it is possible to know joy even when our circumstances are not happy or when our bodies are in pain. When this biblical truth permeates our knowledge—when our discipleship is firmly rooted in the word of God—then for the sake of the future good we are strengthened to say "no" to the present pleasure.

By contrast, a worldview (such as Western materialism that permeates much of American culture) that denies God and any spiritual reality and even denies any meaningful concept of mind (reducing mind to a physical biochemical brain) is left with nothing except body. Joy and happiness in this view are illusory concepts, reducible to mere bodily pleasure. A culture that has bought into this deceptive worldview will therefore become a culture that pursues pleasure above all things: a hedonistic culture consumed by instant gratification.

And this is why having a worldview deeply rooted in the gospel and the word of God is an important part of how God equips us for this battle against sin and temptation. But it is an equipping we must actively participate in. Part of being deeply rooted in the word of God should be a deeper knowledge of the spiritual reality, and the spiritual battle, and the principles mentioned in Hebrews and lived out by Moses: the knowledge of what truly satisfies our longing, in contrast to that which is only fleeting. Furthermore, even Christians who affirm the truth of Scriptures, and a belief in a spiritual reality and the reality of joy, are still bombarded with constant deceits.

We live in a materialistic commercial consumer culture: a culture or economic system predicated on convincing us to purchase material consumer goods, which it does by convincing us through advertisements that these goods or pleasures will satisfy us. Commercials show happy people, with jealous neighbors, living an apparently good and satisfying life, because they have spent money on possessions or pleasures. As I noted, this deceit bombards us almost constantly through all media. Do you want to open yourself up to God's work freeing you from the temptation of the lust of the eyes and the lust of the flesh? Turn off the media and meditate on God's word. To return to our opening chapter, if the time you spend weekly in spiritual formation, and in being shaped by a biblical worldview, is only a small fraction of the time you spend consuming media (whether news media or other forms of entertainment, whether CNN or Fox or you favorite sitcom), then you can't helped but be shaped by that false and damaging worldview.

Knowledge alone isn't enough either—not if we truly desire transformation. And here is where the spiritual disciplines come in, helping open us up to the work of the Holy Spirit. When it comes to the lust of the flesh, the spiritual discipline of fasting may be especially meaningful and freeing. Richard Foster observed, "Fasting helps us keep our balance in life. How easily we begin to allow nonessentials to take precedence in our lives. How quickly we crave things we do not need until we are enslaved by them." Referencing 1 Corinthians 6:12 and 9:27, he goes on to say, "Our human cravings and desires are like a river that tends to overflow its banks; fasting helps keep them in their proper channel."[17] Again, as I have noted, there is nothing sinful about physical pleasure in its "proper channel"; the ability as bodily beings to enjoy bodily pleasure is a good gift from God, as are many of the particular pleasures we feel. Yet it is so easy for pleasures to overflow their channels and for our desires to become our gods. We don't fast from food because food is sinful, but so that we are not enslaved by it. "When the glory of some created thing rules your heart," Paul David Tripp writes, "you will live not for the glory of your Redeemer but for that thing. When love for a certain thing is a more dominant motivator than love for God, you will turn your back on God and as you do, you will step over his boundaries."[18]

As for the lust of the eyes and the desire to possess, the discipline of simplicity, as well as the practice of thankfulness, are particularly relevant. In fact, the spiritual disciplines often work together. (Jan Johnson's *Spiritual Disciplines Companion* study guides even presents them in pairs.) One of the most significant and freeing fasts I ever did for Lent was a fast from all catalogs, including my favorite catalogs for fishing and outdoor gear and apparel. One of my favorite passages in Foster's book is in his chapter on simplicity.

> Because we lack a divine Center our need for security has led us to an insane attachment to things. We must clearly understand that the lust for affluence in contemporary society is psychotic. It is psychotic because it has completely lost touch with reality. We crave things we neither need nor enjoy . . . We are made to feel ashamed to wear clothes or drive cars until they are worn out. The mass media have convinced us that to be out of step with fashion

---

17. Foster, *Celebration of Discipline*, 49.
18. Tripp, *Awe*, 81.

The Lust of the Eyes and Flesh

is to be out of step with reality. It is time we awake to the fact that conformity to a sick society is to be sick. Until we see how unbalanced our culture has become at this point we will not be able to deal with the mammon spirit within ourselves nor will we desire Christian simplicity.[19]

Foster goes on a few pages later to point out how the practice—the spiritual discipline—of simplicity can be freeing. "Simplicity is the only thing that can sufficiently reorient our lives so that possessions can be genuinely enjoyed without destroying us. Without simplicity we will either capitulate to the 'mammon' spirit of this present evil age, or we will fall into an un-Christian legalistic asceticism. Both lead to idolatry. Both are spiritually lethal."[20]

To these I would add the disciplines of hospitality and thankfulness, as well as giving more intentional thought to how we practice the Sabbath and the impact our practices can have on our slavery to consumption.[21] But to reemphasize my earlier point—because it is so important—the path toward transformation and freedom from the chains of these two lusts isn't putting forth a human effort, working really hard to change ourselves by practicing spiritual disciplines. The spiritual disciplines can open us up to God's transforming work in our lives. They can also reveal to us some of the root causes of our weakness and the reasons certain desires hold such power over us. Does our gluttony stem from a simple desire for the physical pleasure of food? Or is it rooted in a lack of trust in God to provide for us? Or is it a way we can take control of our lives when they seem out of control? Likewise, though for some the lust of sexual sin may come from the desire for the physical pleasure, for others it may have more to do with power and control over others.

And thus leads us to the third and final area where the enemy's temptation is often at work.

---

19. Foster, *Celebration of Discipline*, 70.
20. Foster, *Celebration of Discipline*, 74.
21. I highly recommend Norman Wirzba's books *Food and Faith* (which has a chapter on "Saying Grace") and *Living the Sabbath*.

7

Pride of Life

A Threefold Look at Temptation, Part II

> "Yet the way of the Ring to my heart is by pity, pity for weakness and the desire of strength to do good.... I shall have such need of [strength]. Great perils lie before me."
>
> —Gandalf in J. R. R. Tolkien's *The Lord of the Rings*

Persecution, Suffering, and the Gospel of Christ

FOR THE PAST THREE decades, I have taught at a small secular liberal arts college in New England. During that time, I have had several colleagues for whom Christian faith was an important part of their lives: wonderful, thoughtful, compassionate human persons, a few of whom have gone to my own church, and many more who attended a variety of other churches in the area. Nonetheless, the institution has often been a challenging and even hostile place for faculty, staff, and students of committed Christian faith. While that hostility isn't usually directed at those who view their faith as an entirely private subjective matter to be kept out of public discourse, for those who believe the Bible makes objective truth claims or offers transcendent moral teaching, disdain and often outright opposition is a reality.

One year, in the first decade of my career, a Christian student group on campus got in trouble for holding a belief that the Bible—as the word of

Pride of Life

God that spoke truth to our lives—proclaimed moral teaching in the area of sexuality. A student who didn't hold that belief, and who didn't get elected to a position of leadership, complained that he was being discriminated against. The student group was put on probation.

Although I had not been involved in any of the decisions or elections, and didn't learn about the situation until later, as the faculty advisor of the group I was considered guilty by association. One colleague wrote a letter in the campus newspaper saying that I was unfit to be a professor and should be fired. A college administrator called me into his office and spent several minutes chastising me for being affiliated with this Christian group he considered discriminatory. At the end of his lecture, he told me I had no right to affirm any belief system. "All belief systems are equal valid," he said.

That last sentence—a statement both self-contradictory and also intolerant, though wrapped in a veneer of tolerance—was one I wasn't going to let slip past unchallenged. Without much thought to the consequences, I gave the obvious reply: "What about the belief system that not all belief systems are equally valid? Is that a valid belief?"

Of course, if he had answered "yes," he would have had to accept my belief as valid; if he answered "no" then he was acknowledging that not all beliefs are valid. The administrator, perhaps recognizing the self-contradictory nature of his statement, grew red in the face. He turned his back on me for several seconds. Then he finally turned around and gave a noncommittal answer: "I guess so."

The point of the latter story is not to seek sympathy. Despite a few awkward moments, I didn't lose my job. I wasn't demoted or fined or punished in any way. The voices calling for my head faded. Years later, I even developed a friendly relationship with that administrator. Countless Christians throughout the past two millennia have suffered far worse, ranging from far more severe workplace discrimination, to imprisonment, to torture, to death. Nor is my purpose to complain about the opposition to Christianity in our supposedly tolerant but often intolerant secular institutions. I have no desire to rile up Christians with fear or anger in order to oppose that sort of behavior I faced—and that many believers face in our culture today, however hypocritical or unfair it may be. I share that story more as a personal confession. This opposition brought up for me two very different types of temptations, both of which I believe are common for many in the church.

One temptation is to compromise our faith: to distance ourselves from Christianity or privatize our religion: to be secretive or even ashamed of the gospel in order to avoid any threat of persecution or even any loss of our comfort or status. I know I'm not alone in this. I've witnessed Christians slowly move away from church and faith, trying to blend into culture in order to avoid opposition. We might not explicitly deny Christ, but we minimize any visible aspect of our Christian lives that might cause anybody to dislike us. As noted, that remains a temptation for me, particularly in moments when I am concerned for my job and my livelihood.

However a greater (though more subtle) temptation is, I believe, the temptation to fight back against the perceived injustice through the secular power structures of society. Perhaps we lawyer up, and try to sue. Or we bring a big fight through the media. Or maybe we organize boycotts. Often we seek solutions through political power. This second approach may seem more faithful in that it doesn't require us to deny Christ or distance ourselves from church or Christianity. And yet the latter approach of pursuing power to thwart or silence opposition and protect ourselves is, in many ways, rooted in the same basic desire for comfort—or at least a desire to avoid discomfort and suffering. We turn the unfair situation into an us-versus-them battle: a protect-the-rights-of-Christians campaign, which often really means protect the comfort, wealth, and power of Christians within our culture.

About the time I finished up the second draft of this book, and sent it out to a publisher, my wife and I had dinner with some good friends: a couple several years younger than us, who have three young children still at home. The husband had just been diagnosed with cancer. He and his wife were both still processing that information. Yet the husband and father shared something very powerful with me as we sat outside watching the sun set. He told me that fighting the cancer wasn't going to be his top priority. It would be very easy for his life to be consumed with a battle to maintain his health and prosperity as though that were the most important thing in life. It would be very easy to spend so much energy pursuing health that he didn't think about what God might be doing through him and through the cancer and any possible suffering resulting from it.

Pride of Life

Fear and the Pursuit of Power

Of the three temptations that John warns of, I believe the third—"the pride of life," or as the *New American Standard* translation puts it, "the boastful pride of life"—is the most dangerous and destructive both to individual followers of Christ and to the body of Christ as a whole. It is also often the most tempting, and the easiest to justify with religious-sounding language. Eugene Peterson's translation in *The Message* identifies this pride of life as "wanting to appear important," and that is certainly part of it. Yet if we understand this third temptation through the lens of the original sin of Adam and Eve or the temptation of Jesus after his forty-day wilderness fast, it is more than just wanting to appear important; it is a desire for power and authority, at the root of which is a desire to replace God, and to put ourselves on his throne.

This temptation to grasp authority is insidious and pervasive, especially when we defend our power-grasping by claiming some good use of the sought-after power. It may be the most damaging sin of our human race. It is a temptation Satan repeatedly throws at Jesus right up to his final moments on the cross. It comes through the words of the chief priests and teachers of the law as Jesus is dying. "Let this Messiah, this king of Israel, come down now from the cross," they say, "that we may see and believe" (Mark 15:32, NIV). Not only do they suggest that Jesus claim power, but they even suggest a good-sounding reason for him to use that power: by demonstrating divine power to save himself from suffering, Jesus might lead some to faith: to seeing and believing in him as a result of his power. Sounds like a good justification, doesn't it?

Matthew records other passers-by saying similar things: "Those who passed by hurled insults at him, shaking their heads and saying, 'You who are going to destroy the temple and build it in three days, save yourself! Come down from the cross, if you are the Son of God!'" (Matthew 27:39–40, NIV). Here's a chance for Jesus to prove he is the Son of God. Once again, he needs only demonstrate power and he could win souls for God. Again, it sounds like a worthwhile goal.

Making it even more challenging to resist, sometimes the temptation comes through a friend or a fellow member of the church. Jesus' own disciple Peter gives in to the temptation when he tries to protect Jesus by force, cutting off the ear of one of the mob who come to arrest Jesus. Jesus' response suggests this was yet another attempt of Satan to tempt him. "Put your sword away!" he tells Peter. "Shall I not drink the cup the Father has given me?" (John 18:10–11, NIV).

Indeed, a desire for power was a temptation for all of Israel. In the time of Jesus, many in Israel wanted a messiah to establish a worldly kingdom where they—the Israelites, God's people—would be in charge. Similarly, modern churchgoers often want the same thing: for God to establish a worldly kingdom where they wield power and authority. But Jesus came to Israel for a different purpose. Where Peter wanted to choose the sword, Jesus chose the cross.

As I noted earlier in the book, I grew up in the 1960s and 1970s watching a lot of Western movies and television. Although my favorite Western film is *Silverado* (1985), I saw many reruns from the 1950s and 1960s. A classic Western scene shows the heroes in a wagon train getting attacked by bandits. The heroes circle the wagons, get into the proverbial protective ring, and fire shots at the enemy outside. If it isn't a wagon train, it's an old fort, or perhaps a walled town or hacienda. As I've heard it noted more than once—and, unfortunately, all too accurately—the Christian church, crippled by a similar fear, often follows this same model: we circle our wagons and fires shots at the bandits outside.

Even evangelistic efforts within the church often fit this fear-driven circling-the-wagons model. We sit inside our safe circles firing shots at the bandits outside. Except, since we know we should be proclaiming the gospel, every once in a while we try to lasso one of the bandits riding by and drag them into the circle with us. Because, well, it would be scary to actually have to go live among the bandits and get to know them.

I mention fear in addition to power because fear is closely allied with pride, which is the topic of this chapter. In her Renovaré interview with Nathan Foster, Rebecca Konyndyk DeYoung noted how in the spiritual traditions she had been studying, fear is seen as standing alongside pride at the very *root* of the tree that bears the fruit we identify as sin; pride and fear are often the real *sources* of sins that may be manifested in some other outward way, for example as a sin of the flesh. Thus, DeYoung explains, if we address the outward sin without getting at the source, it is like plucking the bad fruit from the branches of a tree without getting rid of the root of the tree; if you do that, the fruit will just grow back.[1]

Explaining this connection between pride and fear, DeYoung notes, "Pride [is] the need to be in control of your own life. Fear is the flip side of

---

1. DeYoung, "Deadly Sins and Their Remedies."

Pride of Life

that: 'I'm afraid I won't be [in control].'"[2] Looking back at my own experiences I shared in an earlier chapter, I think some of my resistance to God's leading that made it difficult for me to give up skiing related to my fears. One fear was that if I gave up skiing I wouldn't be significant anymore as a human person because I wouldn't have anything left in my life I was good at. An even more insidious fear—though I doubt I could have articulated or even recognized it at the time—was that if I obeyed God's calling to give up skiing, then he might ask me to give up something else later. If I gave up control to God in this area, in what other areas of my life might God ask for control next? That was a real fear running through my mind as I struggled to obey. And in one sense, my fear was well-founded. For the answer was *everything*; God wants control in all areas of my life. That, however, should have been reason for joy, not fear.

In any case, the fear I felt made it very difficult for me to obey. DeYoung goes on to explain how fear impacts our behavior, especially with respect to possessions, comfort, and control.

> Fear prompts all kinds of over-grasping, overcompensating for control. . . . One place it shows up probably most obviously is in the area of greed and avarice, because one thing you can control is "stuff." You can go get more stuff and it makes you feel powerful. . . . You're feeling out of control in your life and you go buy something that you can then own and master and be in charge of, it's a little bit of a power trip. It helps . . . makes me feel less afraid because I have control here; I've reasserted mastery over my life.[3]

Listening to this podcast a second time made me think even more about fear, which I already addressed earlier in this book. I can see again why even though it may come in the guise of the church or in biblical-sounding language, inciting fear is counter to biblical teaching.

And this brings us back to the pride of life. Not only is this the third and final temptation John warns about (after the lust of the eyes and the lust of the flesh), but in the garden in Genesis 3, the third aspect of how the serpent uses the fruit to tempt to Eve is also through the promise of power or authority: playing on the desire to be in control—the desire, ultimately, to become gods. Interestingly, Eve expresses this as a desire to gain wisdom, which seems like a much more holy pursuit than power. Wisdom is good, isn't it? Shouldn't we all pursue wisdom? We could say the same thing

---

2. DeYoung, "Deadly Sins and Their Remedies."
3. DeYoung, "Deadly Sins and Their Remedies."

about the Pharisees' reasons for Jesus to demonstrate power by coming off the cross. What if Jesus had just proven his divinity and called upon the power of the angels under his command? Surely such a display of authority would have prompted many to follow him. Likewise for Christians today, the temptation to power often comes wrapped up the guise of something good: some noble end we wish to achieve for which we need more authority or money, or some bad outcome (such as persecution or suffering) we wish to avoid for which we need more power or influence.

The problems, however, are both that a good end does not justify a bad means, and also that it is very easy to deceive ourselves about exactly what our ends are, and to tangle up a seemingly good goal with a bad one. We can affirm that wisdom is a good thing, but the third lust is not just for wisdom; it is for power, both as an end and as a means. And that power seems to be what Eve really wanted. If you think it is an overreach to connect Eve's supposed desire for wisdom with the more insidious desire to become God, you need look only at Satan's words in the previous verse: "For God knows that when you eat from it your eyes will be opened, and *you will be like God*, knowing good and evil" (Genesis 3:5, NIV, emphasis added). This, indeed, is the boastful pride of life: the thought that we can be like gods. The wisdom we should desire is the wisdom to *know* God. The wisdom Eve is tempted by is the wisdom to *be* a god: the wisdom that will grant her power, control, authority.

And as DeYoung notes, the twins of pride and fear may lead to all sorts of other sinful and destructive behaviors. Yet—as with Eve's desire for wisdom—this pride so often comes disguised. Indeed, within the church this desire for power rarely comes with the label *pride* at all; it may even come as a desire for something good (like wisdom), or a desire to have power in order to *do* something good.

Justifying the Pursuit of Power

Let's return again to Eugene Peterson's book *The Jesus Way*, a wealth of wisdom for those who want to be followers of Jesus and his way. In the book, Peterson describes the devil's third temptation of Jesus in the wilderness.

> The third temptation: rule the world. The devil wants us to use Jesus to run the world, take charge of the world—"all the kingdoms of the world and their splendor." What an offer! Who is more qualified? Here is the opportunity to establish a rule of peace

and justice and prosperity. Create a government free of corruption. But of course it would have to be on the devil's terms, a rule conditioned by the unholy *if*—"if you will fall down and worship me." The devil's way would be absolutely perfect in its functions, but with no personal relationships.[4]

What Satan sought to use as a temptation for Jesus remains a temptation for all of us who want to follow Jesus today. We Christians all too often strive to rule the world. We want to take charge, so that we can bring about all sorts of good things we are sure are in keeping with God's plan. If we could just be in power, and impose a Christian morality, we could accomplish the peace, justice, and prosperity that would be good for all. Surely these are worth striving for.

However the pursuit of worldly power—whether political, financial, or cultural—seems always to require compromises, perhaps because the very act of pursuing power for ourselves is a denial of our dependence on God and his power. The nature of worldly power is that it is worldly. It is of the kingdom of this world. Thus to gain that power, we have to follow the principles of the kingdoms of this world, which is to say, the way of the devil. Sadly, the church has all too often been willing to follow the devil's way in order to gain power, and often does it with a justification of the good that can be accomplished: peace, justice, prosperity. Especially prosperity. Power is so much more tempting for the church to pursue when it leads to the comfort, wealth, and ease of those within the church, protecting us from persecution, protecting our jobs and wealth and status. But even when there is no personal gain of prosperity, the pursuit of power using the ways of the world is still the way of the world and not the way of Jesus.

J. R. R. Tolkien and C. S. Lewis were especially good at exposing how this temptation works. In Tolkien's *The Lord of the Rings,* the great battle is against the powerful demonic figure of Sauron who seeks to rule Middle-earth. There is no doubt that battle ought to be waged against Sauron, even as Paul makes it clear in Ephesians that we fight a battle against spiritual wickedness. The wise and heroic figures of Gandalf, Galadriel, Elrond, Aragorn, and Faramir all oppose Sauron, and are willing to sacrifice much—including their own lives—in order to defeat that enemy. Knowing the importance of the war, and the power of the enemy who seeks their destruction, it is therefore a great temptation to all of them to claim the One Ring. It would be easy to justify such a claim. They are all perceived as good

---

4. Peterson, *The Jesus Way,* 33.

and wise, and others trust them, even encouraging them to pursue power and authority. Think of how much good they could do if they claimed the One Ring and wielded its power to defeat Sauron and save Middle Earth—also saving countless lives.

Gandalf articulately identifies the temptation. "Yet the way of the Ring to my heart is by pity, pity for weakness and the desire of strength to do good. . . . I shall have such need of [strength]. Great perils lie before me." Yet despite his desire to do good, Gandalf still recognizes the pursuit of this sort of worldly power as a temptation that would corrupt him if he succumbed. "And over me the Ring would gain a power still greater and more deadly," he says. "Do not tempt me! For I do not wish to become like the Dark Lord himself."[5] He thus refuses to take the ring. Doing so is a great act of humility on his part, which is the opposite of the pride that causes us to grasp at power. Gandalf recognizes that it isn't his role to save the world, and that ultimately he can place his trust in God, the Creator, known in the languages of Middle-earth as Eru (the One) and Ilúvatar (Father of All). Gandalf makes use of the power the creator gave him, but doesn't compromise morally in order to grasp for more power.

Galadriel also recognizes the allure of power. Through her temptation, Tolkien portrays more explicitly the connection between pride and fear. The voice of fear constantly speaks to Galadriel: if Sauron returns to power, she will lose her way of life, her comfort, her authority and autonomy—everything she has worked for in the land of Lothlórien. At one point she says to Frodo, "Do you not see now wherefore your coming is to us as the footstep of Doom?" This sort of fear is often present in the church today. If such and such a person or political power is allowed to take authority, fear tells us, then we (the Christian church) will lose our power, our autonomy, our (usually comfortable) way of life. And maybe that's true. So we grasp for power to prevent it, and justify the compromises along the way. In a recent election, I witnessed Christian friends (of both political parties) using social media to promote stories without any regard to whether they were true in order to promote a particular candidate they thought would bring more power to the Christian church and its agenda. Others were willing to excuse, deny, or even defend immorality in certain candidates whom they wanted to win, again hoping that by putting those candidates in power they would also be giving political power to the church. Again, those

---

5. Tolkien, *The Lord of the Rings,* Book I, Chapter ii.

Pride of Life

compromises seemed motivated by fear: if the other candidate wins then the church will lose some of its political influence, power, and comfort.

Admittedly Galadriel was correct in her assessment of the danger. Thus the temptation, put by the author into her own words, went like this: "And now at last it comes. You will give me the Ring freely! In place of the Dark Lord you will set up a Queen. And I shall not be dark, but beautiful and terrible as the Morning and the Night! Fair as the Sea and the Sun and the Snow upon the Mountain! Dreadful as the Storm and the Lightning! Stronger than the foundations of the earth. All shall love me and despair!"[6] The Western Christian church seems often to say something similar, justifying the little (or not so little) compromises in honesty, or morality, or in the sorts of alliances we make, in order to gain that power to preserve our comfortable way of life.

The wisdom Tolkien portrays through Galadriel and Gandalf, however, is quite different from that of our world. Both of those heroes refuse the temptation to pursue power. Their faith is in a higher power, and that faith enables them to resist fear and pride. So it also is with the human hero Faramir, who explains his own conviction rather simply: "I would not even snare an orc with a falsehood."[7] Even the compromise of a little lie for the sake of winning some battle, however good that battle might be, would be wrong.

And yet it is also tempting. It is the boastful pride of life, the temptation to bite the fruit to be wise, the temptation for Jesus to call upon the angels to rescue him and prove his power. Faramir's brother Boromir gives in to the temptation. Unlike Faramir, he tries to grab after that power. Again, Tolkien gives us Boromir's justification in his own words. Speaking of the One Ring of power, he says:

> "It is a gift, I say; a gift to the foes of Mordor. It is mad not to use it, to use the power of the Enemy against him. The fearless, the ruthless, these alone will achieve victory. What could not a warrior do in this hour, a great leader? What could not Aragorn do? Or if he refuses, why not Boromir? The Ring would give me power of Command. How I would drive the hosts of Mordor, and all men would flock to my banner!"[8]

---

6. Tolkien, *The Lord of the Rings*, Book II, Chapter vii.
7. Tolkien, *The Lord of the Rings*, Book IV, Chapter v.
8. Tolkien, *The Lord of the Rings*, Book II, Chapter x.

Grasp after political or military power to defeat the evil enemy. How tempting it is, indeed. We can easily justify ruthless tactics, including dishonesty, including the very tactics we would have condemned earlier had we seen them in the enemy.

As I noted in my book *A Hobbit Journey*, one principle of Tolkien's heroes who resist fear and pride—and the temptation to power—might be explained like this: It would be better to lose a battle than to defeat your enemy by doing evil; better to lose our worldly possessions, or to suffer bodily harm, than to suffer a moral defeat through moral compromise. Satan is much more interested in leading you into sin than in making you suffer.

C. S. Lewis, in his Narnia stories, shows a biblical wisdom similar to Tolkien's, and illustrates the same fear-driven temptation to pursue power through any means. It is perhaps most poignant in *The Horse and His Boy* when some of the Old Narnians are willing to bring the White Witch back from the dead in order to help defeat King Miraz. They justify raising one evil and immoral ruler to power in order to defeat another ruler they claim is even more immoral. Immorality seems to be justified in the effort to defeat immorality.

Again, such temptations are easier to fall prey to if we have been deceived by the prosperity gospel. If we perceive that health and wealth, or comfort and power, are somehow our right and privilege—that God has promised them to us; that he is a great therapist whose goal is fulfill us and satisfy our desires, rather than to draw us close to him in holiness—then we can give in to the temptation to pursue rule and authority even at the cost of moral compromise.

The Real Threat

What *are* the big threats to Christianity? As I noted earlier, it's not persecution. Persecution may be a threat to our personal comfort and wealth—and maybe even to lives of individual Christians. But persecution isn't actually a threat to the gospel. "I am suffering even to the point of being chained like a criminal," Paul tells Timothy. "But God's word is not chained" (2 Timothy 2:9, NIV). Paul faced tremendous opposition to his work, but he recognized that while he might suffer for his faith as a result of that opposition, God's plan wouldn't be thwarted. Opposition to the gospel message may be a threat to Paul's comfort and livelihood, but it won't imprison or halt God's work.

Note that I'm not saying that I want to suffer or be persecuted. I don't. I like comfort. But the big threat to the Christian church and its witness is compromise, dishonesty, lack of integrity, all of which we are tempted to trade in order to gain power. The New Testament is full of instructions that Christians will suffer, and should be willing to suffer for the kingdom. Its authors also warn us to be sure that when we suffer, it is not because we have done wrong. Near the start of a passage about suffering, Peter writes, "Live such good lives among the pagans that, though they accuse you of doing wrong, they may see your good deeds and glorify God on the day he visits us" (1 Peter 2:12, NIV). Again, from a biblical perspective, it is not persecution that harms the church, but a loss of its witness. Christians should be far more concerned for the integrity of their witness, and for preserving the teachings of the gospel, than for power or comfort, or for social or political agendas and the worldly power to accomplish them. Christians must not live in fear.

This brings me back to my own experiences with which I began this chapter. Many years later, still working at the same college, I had another similar encounter with a different administrator. Applying for a competitive position within the institution, I had to go through a series of interviews. In one interview, an administrator suggested I was unfit for the position explicitly *because I was a Christian*. She questioned whether, as a Christian, I would be able to have sympathy for anybody who wasn't a Christian, and intimated that I would be judgmental. I've been on enough hiring committees to know that for her even to raise the issue of my religion was against the law. There are a whole series of topics we are not allowed to address when hiring. Religion is one of them. And it certainly did cross my mind that, if I were not hired, I could probably successfully sue the college.

And what would that have gained? Might I have made some sort of legal point? Possibly. Could I have won? Likely. Won what? Money, and thus comfort, and maybe some form of power. But what would such a battle have done for my witness and testimony? What would it have accomplished for the kingdom of God? Even had I won some significant monetary award, that sort of us-versus-them battle, perceived as yet more whining by Christians more concerned with their rights than with anything else, would likely have done irreparable damage to any witness I had cultivated over the years. The prosperity offered by my job should not be my highest priority.

Gaining political, legal, or financial power over those who oppose the gospel is not a strategy suggested in the New Testament. Christ, and his apostles who gave us the New Testament made it clear that if we sought to follow Christ we would face persecution. They also made it clear that the persecution in and of itself was not a threat to God's kingdom work. Opposition from the outside is *not* what Paul worried about in his letter to Timothy. Bad teaching within the church is the threat, not attacks from without. The real concern is when the church loses its witness and integrity.

Those who have read C. S. Lewis's Narnia stories know that Lewis understood this well. Narnia is not ultimately destroyed by an external threat, but by a false Aslan; a false religion within Narnia in which leaders pursue power and comfort and the poor are oppressed eventually leads the citizens of Narnia to reject the real Aslan.

Understanding and recognizing this can help. It is a start. Rooting ourselves firmly in the word of God helps us expose the deceits that lead to temptation. Disciple makers need to teach and model these principles, rather than the principles of Western consumerism that promote power, or possession of worldly goods, or enjoyment of physical pleasure as the highest good.

We need to be transformed.

Submission, Service, and Secrecy

One of many insightful observations Jan Johnson makes in her book on spiritual disciplines relates to power. The passage immediately follows one I quoted earlier about God's desire to transform our souls. "As we connect with God, we gradually begin acting more like Christ," she states. What does that transformation look like? The next two sentences give part of the picture. "We become more likely to weep over our enemies instead of discrediting them. We're more likely to give up power instead of taking control." Johnson concludes the paragraph citing Colossians 1:27. "This transformation of our souls through the work of the Holy Spirit results in 'Christ in you, the hope of glory.'"[9] Note that this did not come from a book about power or even a chapter on power. It comes from a book on spiritual disciplines and God's transformational work in our lives through his Holy Spirit. In that sense it is almost an offhand comment. Yet it is telling that one of the first evidences Johnson recognizes of the fruit of the Holy Spirit and the transformational impact of our growth in Christ through the practice of disciplines is the giving up of power. This is, indeed, Christlikeness. To be

9. Johnson, *Spiritual Disciplines Companion*, 7.

Pride of Life

Christlike in our daily lives is to "give up power instead of taking control" even when we feel so well justified grasping control. This very difficult. As noted throughout this chapter, grasping for power is the way of the world, and the church often imitates this way, rather than the way of Christ, and then seeks to justify it.

As with the previous temptations of the lusts of eyes and flesh, the practice of the spiritual disciplines can also help open us up to God's transforming work. All of the disciplines are helpful. When I think of the sin of pride, however, I think especially of disciplines of submission and service, and what Johnson refers to as secrecy: the practice of not letting our acts of service be known. Maybe part of that is the personal conviction I experienced in our recent small group study of the discipline of secrecy. A little later in his book, in his chapter "Service and Secrecy," Johnson quotes from Richard Foster in his explanation of what secrecy looks like and why it is important:

> Service, as a spiritual discipline, is doing good for others with no thought of ourselves.... But if our service is considered successful, we can become wrapped up in ourselves or in the service. That's why secrecy is a twin discipline of service. We refrain from letting our good deeds be known and keep our selves "hidden with Christ in God" (Colossians 3:3). Says Richard Foster, "Hiddenness is a rebuke to the flesh and can deal a fatal blow to pride."[10]

Even when my motives for service may have been good, how desperately in my pride I want others to know about how good that service was, and how wonderful my motives were. It is only a small step from there to a corruption of the motives themselves. My pride is just one facet of that "boastful pride of life" that pushes me to want to be a god through pursuit of power, fame, or glory—or even through pursuit of good things through wrong means. I need transformation.

As with service, the practice of submission also helps open the path to free us from the pursuit of power and authority. "I said that every Discipline has its corresponding freedom," Richard Foster writes. "What corresponds to submission? It is the ability to lay down the terrible burden of always needing to get our own way. The obsession to demand that things go the way we want them to go is one of the greatest bondages in human society today."[11]

10. Johnson, *Spiritual Disciplines Companion*, 47.
11. Foster, *Celebration of Discipline*, 97.

One more example from the J. R. R. Tolkien's *The Lord of the Rings* may help. Samwise Gamgee, the faithful companion of Frodo, is one of only two characters in the history of Middle-earth to freely give up the One Ring, resisting its temptation to power. As far as the histories tell us, he is the only one to do so completely on his own, without great encouragement (bordering on coercion) from Gandalf. Maybe Sam was able to do this because he was a gardener, used to caring for earth, trained with the attitude of a farmer we addressed in an earlier chapter. Or maybe it was because he was a servant, with the heart and attitude of a servant. Tolkien describes the moment as follows:

> In that hour of trial it was the love of his master that helped most to hold him firm; but also deep down in him lived still unconquered his plain hobbit-sense: he knew in the core of his heart that he was not large enough to bear such a burden, even if such visions were not a mere cheat to betray him. The one small garden of a free gardener was all his need and due, not a garden swollen to a realm; his own hands to use, not the hands of others to command.[12]

Samwise would be a good model for followers of Christ today, who seem discontent with the gardens God has given them, and would prefer to rule entire realms.

Jesus is an even better model. Many—indeed the vast majority—of the Israelites of his day rejected Jesus. They wanted a messiah who would be a military or political leader to put them back into power: restore their way of life where they could be in charge, imposing their religious rule rather than being imposed upon by the government of Rome. Jesus didn't come to claim political power. Though he, alone of all humans who have ever lived, could have ruled perfectly, he eschewed power and did not impose his will or order. He didn't come to rule but to serve.

We are called to imitate Christ. The practice of serving, rather than seeking power, is perhaps the best way we can do that. And this leads us to our final section of this chapter.

Discipleship and the Mind-Set of Christ

Ending our look at temptation with an entire chapter on the pursuit of power serves two purposes, though only as I came to the end of this book

---

12. Tolkien, *The Lord of the Rings,* Book IV, Chapter i.

did I see them. One purpose is that the pursuit of power and authority, and its twin root of fear—what John refers to as the "boastful pride of life"—is, I believe, the most damaging of the three temptations. It is often at the root of the other two temptations, and moreover can be far more destructive to the witness of the Christian church than even the lust of the flesh. I believe one of the central causes for the exodus of many young people away from the church today is not the temptation to pursue pleasure in the world, but rather a sort of disgust at the way the church, church-related institutions, church leaders, and many church attendees have pursued power, comfort, and wealth.

An even more important purpose, though, comes from looking at the opposite side of pride and the ungodly pursuit of power and authority: what we might label as humility and corresponding submission. Transformation is central to discipleship and disciple making. Transformation into what? Into Christlikeness. And at the very center of that Christlikeness, according to Paul, is humility and submission. Eschewing the pursuit of power—showing obedience in our imitation of Christ—may be the most important act of discipleship. It is also the hardest.

It is difficult not to be drawn to the icons of power of this world. Even if we recognize these icons as corrupt and immoral, we still are drawn to what they can accomplish (and perhaps also to their wealth and comfort). In fact, the lifestyles and accomplishments of the powerful may be far more appealing to imitate than the example of Jesus. Eugene Peterson, in *The Jesus Way*, contrasts Herod with Jesus. He mentions numerous things Herod accomplished as a political figure who knew how to claim and wield power, ruling Palestine for thirty-four years and completing a long list of magnificent projects including a new temple in Jerusalem. That temple, and all the other wealth that came into the city, must have made the Jewish religious leaders of Herod's day happy with him, despite his immorality—and happy, perhaps, to keep him in power, even though he "was not a religious man." Peterson confesses, therefore, that "it's impossible, at least for me, not to be impressed with Herod."[13] So, too, is it easy for Christians to be impressed with political leaders and figures of power in our world today—and with all that they can accomplish, through their power. We might even be jealous. If they build us a new church building, or help keep religious leaders in positions of seeming power, or protect us from persecution (even while

---

13. Peterson, *The Jesus Way*, 202.

they purposely seek to increase our fear of persecution), then perhaps we want to support them.

However, Peterson goes on to make the crucial point. "And here is the astonishing thing: Jesus ignored the whole business. Jesus spent his life walking down roads and through towns dominated by Herod's policies, buildings shaped by Herod's power, communities at the mercy of Herod's whims. And he never gave them the time of day."[14] Part of the reason, I think, is that Jesus knew where real power comes from, and he wasn't deceived by the semblances of human power of wealth or politics, and so he didn't bow before it. Those who want to follow Jesus should thus consider imitating him in this way also. Do we imitate Herod and his pursuit and use of worldly power to accomplish our agenda? Or perhaps imitate the Pharisees and other religious leaders of Herod's day in using and supporting Herod to accomplish their ends? Or do we imitate Christ?

How about those trying to be disciples of Christ by being disciple makers? What does the witness of our lives and words tell those around us? If others imitate us, will they be imitating Christ because we ourselves are imitating Christ? Or imitating the world, because we imitate the world?

In considering that question, I end this chapter not with Paul's letter to Timothy, but with a passage from the second chapter of his letter to the Philippian church:

> 5 In your relationships with one another, have the same mind-set as Christ Jesus:
>
> 6 Who, being in very nature God,
>
> did not consider equality with God something to be used to his own advantage;
>
> 7 rather, he made himself nothing
>
> by taking the very nature of a servant,
>
> being made in human likeness.
>
> 8 And being found in appearance as a man,
>
> he humbled himself
>
> by becoming obedient to death—
>
> even death on a cross!
>
> 9 Therefore God exalted him to the highest place
>
> and gave him the name that is above every name,
>
> 10 that at the name of Jesus every knee should bow,

---

14. Peterson, *The Jesus Way*, 202.

in heaven and on earth and under the earth,
11 and every tongue acknowledge that Jesus Christ is Lord,
to the glory of God the Father. (Philippians 2:5–11, NIV)

8

A Short Conclusion

"But What Do I Actually Do to Make Disciples?"

WHEN I FINISHED AN earlier draft of this book containing only the first seven chapters, I shared it with a few friends—all fellow writers whom I also admired for their thoughtful faith—and asked for critique on both the writing and the spiritual content. How might I improve the book? What are the flaws? Is it worth publishing?

One of these readers, in addition to a few style suggestions to help with readability, also expressed interest in one significant addition: he wanted a chapter to "flesh out more of the how-tos." He regularly meets with a group for Bible study and mutual encouragement toward the goal of growing more like Christ. He wondered what, practically speaking, they could do in response to this book. "What does your manuscript say to that group?" he asked. "What is one thing you would like . . . to change in how we think or do in connection with each other?"

Although I was thankful for his suggestions on the first seven chapters—and I did my best to follow through on them—I hesitated to take his last suggestion of a "how-to" chapter. As with many endeavors in the Christian walk, it is often a temptation to turn disciple making from something personal and relational into something formulaic or institutional. Somebody takes one particular experience of disciple making (which perhaps worked well in their given situation) and makes a program out of it. They turn disciple making into a sequence of prescribed steps, implicitly (and

A Short Conclusion

possibly even explicitly) communicating that all disciple-making efforts and activities look like that (and only like that).

One of the central themes to much of the writings of Eugene Peterson—an aspect of his books that make them so important in our present day, and so relevant and challenging for me—is his emphasis on not depersonalizing ministry. He repeatedly warns against abstractions and strategies that become impersonal. In *Tell It Slant*, he writes,

> There is nothing quite as destructive to the gospel of Jesus Christ as the use of language that dismisses the way Jesus talks and prays, and takes up instead the rhetoric of smiling salesmanship or vicious invective. If, in the name of Jesus, truth is eviscerated into facts, salvation depersonalized into a strategy, or love abstracted into a slogan or principle, the gospel is blasphemed.[1]

Similarly, in *The Jesus Way*, in addressing the three wilderness temptations of Jesus, Peterson illuminates the contrast between the incarnation of Jesus and the strategies of the devil:

> The devil's temptation strategy is to depersonalize the ways of Jesus but leave the way itself intact. His strategy is the same with us. But a way that is depersonalized, carried out without love or intimacy or participation, is not, no matter how well we do it, no matter how much good is accomplished, the Jesus way. . . . The devil is the consummate ideologue, but he is incapable of incarnation. He uses people to embody his projects in functional rather than personal relationships. The devil is the ultimate in disincarnation. Every time that we embrace ways other than the ways of Jesus, try to manipulate people or events in ways that short-circuit personal relationships and intimacies, we are doing the devil's work.[2]

Sadly, the depersonalizing strategies Peterson warns about—strategies that replace love and intimacy with mere programs and projects—are often easier approaches. They can even appear outwardly successful if our goal has to do with numbers of people (or numbers of dollars in coffers). Returning to Alan Jacobs's quote I began this book with, if success means having lots of occasional church goers without concern for whether they are deeply formed by Christian teaching, then a formulaic approach might work just fine and can thus quickly become a default approach.

---

1. Peterson, *Tell It Slant*, 220.
2. Peterson, *The Jesus Way*, 36.

This has certainly happened in disciple making. Many readers of this book who have grown up in the church have probably witnessed something like that at one time or another. In one small group I am a part of in my home church, we have joked that disciple-making relationships need to involve meeting for coffee on Monday afternoons at 3 PM, as though that were somehow the magic formula for success. This depersonalization has caused some in the church to be wary of the word *discipleship* and even the concept.

This is an important message for me to hear and dwell on. I earned a PhD in computer science, with an emphasis on the theoretical side of the field. I am comfortable with abstractions. I have written and taught about Christian apologetics, making regular use of philosophical arguments for the Christian faith. In the family I grew up in, we often wrestled with big theological or moral questions. And there isn't anything fundamentally wrong with ideas, theologies, or abstractions in and of themselves. Much of this book could be seen as an exploration of theological principles. The abstractions only become wrong when they become more important than real persons, as in when a apologetic argument or a theological abstraction or a ministry strategy becomes more real than the individual person I am ministering to or interacting with. To draw upon a famous passage from Paul's letter to the Corinthian church (1 Corinthians 13:2), I can have all the abstract knowledge of the world and affirm all the correct principles, but if I don't have love then that knowledge is nothing.

This is precisely why over the first several chapters of this book, rather than trying to describe one specific set of actions that all disciple makers should follow, I sought to focus on the important ideas and goals of disciple making while leaving freedom to individuals to live those out in different ways and different contexts. Disciple making needs to be rooted in the word of God. It is relational. It is done in the context of the church. And it involves transformation that only comes as a result of God's power at work within us. Yet different disciple-making relationships at different times and places involving different people may look very different even when drawing upon the same principles.

Yet I also appreciated my friend's question, and his corresponding suggestion. I could see where he was coming from. One of the starting points of this book was the recognition that discipleship involves both thinking and acting: both knowing Christ and obeying Christ—"thought accompanied by endeavor," as noted in the Vine's definition of "disciple" I referred to earlier in the first chapter of this book. Disciple making involves not only teaching the gospel, but also modeling that faith. If this book is just an intellectual exercise that doesn't impact our endeavors as disciples and disciple makers, than it accomplishes nothing.

I also knew that, in making that suggestion, my friend was not at all looking to depersonalize disciple making. He wasn't asking for a formula. To the contrary, in suggesting this chapter he wasn't thinking of abstractions at all, but of a *particular* group of people he knows *personally*. This friend cares deeply about love and intimacy and real relationships.

So—as you have probably guessed by the fact that this chapter exists— I decided to follow his last and more challenging suggestion.

Intentionality (and Some Personal Examples)

My first and most important point is that all believers ought to be intentional about disciple making. What is one thing I would like to change in how readers think or what they do in connection with each other? I would like them all to recognize that Christ calls us all to a ministry of making disciples. That is the Great Commission. Whatever that may end up looking like, it ought to be an intentional part of our lives and our discipleship to Christ.

What does that intentionality look like? As the previous section should make clear, it does *not* mean that we have a program and are always looking to plug people into our program. But it does suggest a few specific practical things we might do. First and foremost, disciples of Christ can be regularly praying that God would reveal those relationships that we might invest more time and energy into: those people whom God might be leading us walk alongside as we seek to follow the great disciple-making commission. And then we need to actually keep our eyes and ears open for God's answer, and be ready to act on it. It might seem awkward at first. Satan does not want us to be involved in making disciples, and will throw all sorts of excuses and obstacles across our paths to thwart our obedience—including what for many Christians is the biggest obstacle of them all: bad past experiences with something that somebody called "discipleship." We must remember, though, that it is God's plan and not our own. It is not prideful to think we can be involved in disciple making when that is precisely what God calls his disciples to do. Rather, it is prideful to think that we can follow our own plan, instead of God's.

While it is a certainly a mistake to think that we will reach some point in our walk of faith that we have it all together and can stop growing, it is also a mistake to think that because we are still growing as disciples ourselves we aren't ready to be involved in making disciples. The goal of discipleship is growing closer to Christ and becoming more Christlike. Thus the goal of disciple making is helping others grow closer to Christ and become more Christlike. Although discipleship is a lifetime process, and continues on even for the most mature followers of Christ, a big part of disciple making is therefore the work of evangelism: helping lead others into that relationship with Christ. Again, although as I have already noted early in the book, the Great Commission transcends evangelism—it is about making disciples and not just making converts—evangelism is nonetheless a significant part of disciple making. And some of the most effective evangelists (and thus disciple makers) I have known or seen have been brand new believers who have shared with authenticity and enthusiasm their new faith in and relationship with Christ. No matter where we are in our walk of faith, there will always be others we can help lead closer to Christ.

One thing that makes these new believers such wonderful disciple-making evangelists is their authenticity and genuineness. The fear many have about being intentional in disciple making is that it feels inauthentic—and might comes across that way. I get that. Ultimately, however, as with almost anything we do, when we practice intentionality in disciple making, it becomes a natural part of our character; it becomes a way of life. But if inauthenticity, or becoming formulaic or programmatic, are concerns, remember that the antidote to these problems is love. Even as you pray for those in whose lives God might be calling you to invest, pray also for a genuine love and concern for those same people. Love, even more than obedience to the Christ's commission, should motivate us to seek the spiritual growth of those we know and to be willing to invest in that growth as disciple makers.

If there is one disadvantage to the fact that my initial experience with intentional discipleship (as a recipient in a disciple-making relationship) was such a positive one, it is that I was easily tempted to make all disciple-making relationships look like my first one. I probably tried to do that for several years. Fortunately, I have been blessed by many other relationships that have helped form me as a disciple of Christ and yet looked quite different. Indeed, that continues to be the case, since that process of disciple making in me is far from complete!

A Short Conclusion

The disciple-making relationship Doug had with me was intentional on both of our parts. He was intentional about discipling me, and I was intentional about being discipled by Doug. Since that time, I have been involved as disciple maker in several relationships—often with college students—in which I was intentional about disciple making in the time I spent with them, and they were intentional in looking to me as a spiritual mentor or model. Often they were in a Bible study I was leading, and we spent time together in that study and also outside of the study having meals, or ministering together. Sometimes they helped me co-lead a Bible study for younger students or for those whose Christian faith was newer, and I was able to see a third generation past mine: the things they were hearing from me, they were helping to pass on. In the best of those relationships, I often learned as much from those I was discipling as I was able to pass on to them. Yet there was still something of a mentorship or even father-son aspect to those relationships.

With many students over the years, however, the relationship has been less intentional on their parts. That doesn't mean that I was less intentional. I may still have been seeking to provide an example of the Christian walk and to offer biblically rooted teaching, but the students might not have acknowledged any sort of need or desire for that (at least from me). That is, they might have appreciated something I was offering, but perhaps not identified it as discipleship. I suppose it was a sort of *stealth* disciple making. Some of those relationships eventually developed into deeper ones. Many did not.

Remember that in Pauls' exhortation to Timothy that was the focus of the first several chapters of this book, he tells Timothy to entrust the gospel to *faithful* followers. One of the things I look for when considering what relationships God might be leading me to invest more time in is this question of faithfulness. Are the would-be disciples interesting in growing? Are they willing to take steps toward that growth? Seeing that sort of spiritual fruit may be one of the indications of a relationship I ought to continue to pour myself into. On a flip side, a lack of interest or willingness on the part of somebody else to grow as a disciple does not mean I stop caring about the other person, and it certainly doesn't mean they aren't important to God, but it might mean that it isn't the right time in that person's life, or perhaps that I am not the person God has chosen to do the work of disciple making in that particular relationship, and it may be a time for me to invest less effort there and more in a different relationship.

It is also worth noting that not all of my disciple-making relationships have been with younger people. Early in my career as a college professor, I began and led a Bible study on campus for other faculty and staff, all of whom were actually older than I was. For the first few years, one of the regular faithful attendees was a retired professor who happened to be older even than my parents. He had been a regular church attendee for most of his life. Yet a few months into the study he acknowledged that our study was the first time in his entire life he had ever actually read and studied the Bible with the question of how it applied to his life. All his previous explorations of Scripture had been merely academic exercises looking at cultural or historical contexts. Now he was looking at the Bible with me, and we were asking together what it meant to be disciples of Christ. He was seeking to apply what he learned to how he lived. Though he was considerably older than I was, and in many ways far more knowledgeable and experienced, I was intentionally doing the work of disciple making in his life.

I have also been intentional in seeking to *be* discipled. I have learned much from others who have made a lifetime habit of disciple making. Throughout much of my adult life I have been fortunate to find faithful, mature believers from whom I could learn and whose lives I sought to imitate. Three in particular that come to mind are Dick and Mardi Keyes (for many years the leaders of the L'Abri community in Massachusetts) and the late Eugene Peterson. There have been several others I would mention if I had more space.

On numerous occasions I've been fortunate to have heard Dick or Mardi Keyes speak. Thus even if I had never had the joy of a personal relationship with them, I would have learned a tremendous amount from their thoughtful, articulate explorations and examinations of the Christian faith and all its implications. Some of Dick's books are among the most important, most often read, and most often recommended books on my shelf. One of the central principles I repeatedly heard from them is that there is no sacred-secular dichotomy in life: we cannot divide life into sacred things (like prayer, worship, church, and Bible reading) and secular things (like work, gardening, changing diapers, washing dishes, and navigating traffic); all of life is sacred, meaning that it all should be put under the authority of Christ. That teaching has meant far more to me because I got to know Dick and Mardi personally and saw that important biblical principle lived out daily in their lives. When I've sat down to a meal with them, or just enjoyed a cup of tea in their homes, their first questions for me were always about

A Short Conclusion

my family, and how I was doing, and what was going on in my life. They demonstrated a real care for me as a person. If our conversations turned to questions of theology, philosophy, culture, or ministry—and they often did—that personal relationship was there as a foundation.

I also learned a great deal from watching Dick speak—not just the ideas he shared and how he presented them, but the patient way he responded to questions, and how he treated people before and after his talks. He always communicated to members of his audience, even those vehemently disagreeing with him, that they were important and that he cared about people more than about abstractions. Interestingly, it was Ben Keyes, one of Dick and Mardi's sons—well-discipled by his parents, I'm sure—who lovingly and gently offered me one of the most important corrections I've received in my own life as a writer and public speaker, pointing out a bad habit I had of getting so caught up in the ideas I was presenting that I sometimes interrupted people asking questions by starting to answer them before they had finished rather than hearing them out completely.

Though Eugene Peterson was roughly the age of my father, I was fortunate also to have him as a friend and mentor for several years. In 2007, I was invited to join the Chrysostom Society, a small group of writers of Christian faith, of which Eugene and his wife Janice had been members for many years. I met Eugene before I had read any of his writings except for a few passages of his popular Bible translation *The Message*—which it would have been hard to avoid, given how often it was quoted in churches or conferences I'd attended. So, while I knew of him by reputation, I didn't know anything about him as a person, or about his life, or even about his many books. The first year I was part of the gathering, I had only casual contact with him over meals and various activities during the day. I think I felt intimidated to initiate conversation with him. It turned out that was a foolish feeling. Both Eugene and Janice proved humble and approachable, personable, encouraging, and also very humorous. Indeed, I can't think of anybody I've ever met with a warmer or more sincere and welcoming smile and corresponding personality than Eugene. Although I can't remember Eugene ever teasing me, Janice often did in a good-natured way: the way I imagined she might tease one of her own sons. And, in fact, they both told me more than once that I reminded them of one of their sons. In a spiritual sense, I certainly was.

Although different members of the Chrysostom Society often meet or collaborate in various locations through the year, the entire group gathers only once a year for a three-night weekend. Those annual gatherings, and two times I visited the Petersons at their home in Montana, were my only opportunities to spend time with Eugene and Jan. I can't claim to have known them well. And yet they have had a profound influence on my life. It wasn't long after meeting Eugene—hearing him lead our small gathering in morning or evening devotions, or deliver a Sunday morning homily to us, or especially just sitting in conversation listening to him tell stories about his life or ask me questions about mine—that I was motivated to start reading his books. I began with *A Long Obedience in the Same Direction,* and such was its profound impact on me that I didn't stop until I had devoured another five of his books and passed them on to as many people as I could. My recommendation always came with the message that Eugene was *real*: that the words in his books were echoed by the actions of his life. His teaching about a life following Christ is certainly profound enough and well-enough written that his books alone would have been significant. The title of that first book of his that I read could capture the intent of the Great Commission, and the command not just to make converts but to make disciples who obey. Yet his life shared with me in relationship has greatly increased the impact of his disciple making in my life. The things I have heard from him in the presence of witnesses are things I now hope to entrust to others.

I remember two occasions in particular. The first was a two-hour car ride with Jan and Eugene back to the airport at the end of one of our weekends. We spent much of that time talking about the *Chronicles of Narnia* and C. S. Lewis's literary and theological imagination. At the time, I think Eugene was rereading the Narnia stories. Although I was relatively unknown as an author, he seemed to take my thoughts very seriously. That he did so was a tremendous encouragement to me. I suppose it also bore witness to his own humility and eagerness to continue learning.

The second memory that stands out was of an evening at one of our gatherings, after all the formal activities of the day had come to an end. Eugene sensed that I was discouraged. He spent some quiet time with me talking and listening and encouraging. He also exhorted me to publish a particular essay I had written that he thought was good and true and important, but also one that we both expected would ruffle some feathers. In fact, even as he was encouraging me, he was also exhorting me not to act in fear, especially when it came to handling the word of God correctly. I took

A Short Conclusion

his exhortation and published the essay, and it turned out our expectations were correct.

As far as I knew, neither the Keyes nor the Petersons would have explicitly identified their relationship with me as one of disciple making—though on the other hand, as mature Christians devoted to a life of discipleship to Christ, I know that disciple making was a way of life for both of them and all the principles of this book flowed naturally out of that in their lives. Which is to say, at some level they probably have understood that all our relationships are part of the important work of making disciples, or have the potential to be so, and thus every word we speak should reflect biblical truth, and every deed we do should take into consideration who we are imitating—namely Christ—so that others who imitate us are also imitating Christ.

A Few Final Thoughts: Four Repeated Principles in Practice, and One New One

Hopefully—although I deliberately avoided offering a specific list of things one ought to do in a disciple-making relationship—the previous section provided some further insights. Most important among them is prayer shaped by intentionality. Or, perhaps we should say intentionality shaped by prayer. Continuing to mine that same vein of ore, following are a few more thoughts based on the four principles outlined earlier in this book (though not in the same order) plus one more principle, perhaps the most important and most practical one of the book.

Disciple making needs to be rooted in the word of God. What does that mean in practice? It might be worked out in any of several ways. A small group Bible study is one obvious context for disciple-making relationships. Jesus traveled with a small group, and taught them regularly. Those disciples heard the word of God straight from God! I suppose the importance of Jesus teaching to a small group could be considered in the light of efficiency: leading a small group Bible study offers the opportunity to teach several people at once, rather than repeating the same teaching over and over to different individuals. Although it is easy in our modern world obsessed with efficiency—in manufacturing, agriculture, and even in our fast-food dining—to place too much emphasis on being efficient at the cost of other more important values, efficiency isn't in and of itself bad; Jesus had limited time, and so do we. Teaching a dozen people together in his small group meant he could pass on his teaching to more people during his lifetime.

Though "small" is an important word here, since being relational is also one of the principles of disciple making, and a group that gets too large makes real relationships difficult or impossible. Even Jesus limited the size of his small group of disciples to twelve, and for most of the rest of us even twelve is likely too large a group. He certainly taught large crowds at times, and also interacted at more personal levels with many others outside his most famous small group—for example, his friends Mary and Martha and Lazarus (see Luke 10:38–42 and John 11), as well as Nicodemus the Pharisee (see John 3), and even Zacchaeus the tax collector (see Luke 19:1–10). Yet he spent the most intimate time with that group of twelve, teaching and at times admonishing them. He also involved them in his ministry activities, and occasionally sent them out to minster without him as opportunities for them to grow and be stretched. The four Gospels are full of these accounts.

Another advantage of a small group is that it gives opportunities for the disciples, who all listened to the same teaching together, to discuss that teaching among themselves and thus strengthen and encourage each other, and hold each other accountable. Keep in mind that disciple making in the context of Christian community is itself an important principle to which we will soon return. So I suspect Jesus—and the rabbinical tradition he followed—had many reasons for having and traveling with a small group of disciples.

A small group is not the only way to remain biblically focused, however. A scripturally focused disciple-making relationship many be centered on one-on-one interactions and conversation about the Scriptures, and what they mean, and how they apply. It might involve digging in together to look at some of the more challenging passages of Scripture. It may involve covering some of the more basic tenets of the Christian life. It might come from a mutual question of interest, or area of concern that enables us to look closely together at the teachings of the Bible. It might be rooted in a shared experience, such as being a parent, or a spouse, or caring for an aging parent, or working at the same company. These types of relationships can often form when somebody comes with a question or even a frustration with the Bible over some difficult or troublesome issue, to which we might respond—not with defensiveness—but with a simple invitation to explore the passage or the topic together.

A Short Conclusion

Centering disciple making on God's word doesn't even necessarily come from any mutual agreement to do so, or any explicit opening up of God's word for study. In other words, you don't have to carry a Bible around. This is true especially in the evangelistic side of disciple making. There are many misconceptions about what the Bible teaches. Our friendships and relationships of trust, listening, and respect with those who don't share our Christian faith can offer opportunities to gently correct those misunderstandings with a truer picture of God's word, and that is part of the work of disciple making.

One more important aspect of centering our disciple making on the word of God: study, meditation, and practice of the Bible is not just something we do in relationship with others and when we are meeting with others either in small groups or individually; it must be something central to our own lives whether we are in active moments of disciple making or not. You will not be effective in passing on the word of God as Paul was with Timothy, and Timothy was with his church at Ephesus, unless you root yourself in the word, reading it, studying it, meditating upon it, and living it daily so that it flows out of you.

Another of the principles from Paul's letter is that disciple making takes place in the context of Christian fellowship; it happens in the presence of many witnesses; it is connected to church community in the sense of the church universal, and especially benefits from connectedness to the local church. This is another reason why a small group can be a wonderful context for disciple making. As noted above, a small group provides that Christian fellowship, the presence of witnesses. It's especially fruitful when disciple-making relationships offer the opportunity to worship together and minister together in a local church, both to have some shared experiences and also to increase opportunity for time together.

My experience is that ministries of a local church offer wonderful opportunities for disciple making. It may be obvious that a youth leader is in disciple-making relationships with the youth, or that in a large church with a staff team a senior pastor has opportunity to disciple the rest of the staff as well as the lay leaders of the church such as the elders or deacons. But all ministries of church can be a context for disciple making—though sadly in some churches these opportunities simply turn into places to exercise authority, rather than opportunities for loving and caring interpersonal disciple making. For example, a worship team leader with a team of musicians has a wonderful opportunity not just to make sure the guitarist is holding to the right dynamics and that the harmonies of the vocalists sound good, but also to spend time in encouragement and teaching with the members of that team. The same can be said of church missions trips, and even (perhaps especially) opportunities for service within the church, whether preparing meals for fellowship or doing maintenance work on a building or grounds. These are chances for disciple-making relationships through conversation and co-laboring.

Not all disciple making need take part with everybody involved in the same church, however. A local body is important, but it is not the only aspect of Christian community. Campus ministries or workplace groups can also be fruitful places for discipleship. On the evangelism side of disciple making, it is likely that the person to whom we are ministering does not go to church at all. In the former case, fellowship with other believers is still happening. In the case of evangelism, it is important that those involved in that work are supported by their church community. Indeed, here I would caution that while we hope that our evangelistic efforts may be a part of someone's journey toward Christ that will in turn lead to their involvement in the community of church and God's people, it is a mistake trying to force an unbeliever to attend church in order to hear the message. Jesus dined with Zacchaeus when Zacchaeus was still a tax collector. He didn't require Zacchaeus to come to the temple to meet him. Neither did Peter require the Athenian philosophers (in Acts 17) to come to a Jewish synagogue to hear about Christ; he spoke to them in the marketplace. Fear may prompt a circle-the-wagons mentality toward evangelism where Christians keep themselves cloistered from the hostile world out there, and occasionally seek to snag or lasso an unwary passerby and drag them into our midst. Though it may seem safer, that is not a Christian view of evangelism and not what is meant by the principle that disciple making happens in the context of Christian community.

Church may not be the right place for most evangelistic efforts. Our church community and its gathered worship is, however, a vitally important part of our spiritual growth and transformation. Spiritual transformation—the movement away from rebellion and toward being Christlike—is the goal of discipleship and of disciple making, and it is a work God does in us. Transformation comes as a result of God's power at work within us. Much of that happens when we open ourselves up to God's work in us through his body: through gathered worship together, through the way that Christians sharpen each other, through the teachings and prayer and mutual support

A Short Conclusion

and encouragement, and even—perhaps especially—through the conflicts that arise in church as a bunch of sinners try to do the hard work of forming a body and community. Learning to love each other, which is possibly only through the Holy Spirit, is transformative.

If you want to live out a life inspired by the Great Commission, then be involved in a local church and allow God's transformative work in your life. Commit yourself also to the daily practice of listening to God, and to the practice of spiritual disciplines described earlier in this book. (Spend a month or two or three reading and practicing Richard Foster's book *The Celebration of Discipline*.)

And this brings us, lastly, to the relational aspect—and what that might look like practically in our disciple making, which in turn leads to yet a fifth principle that flows out of it.

Disciple making is, indeed, relational and personal and rooted in love. And all relationships are different. There is no one-size-fits-all model for what a disciple-making relationship looks like. The father-son metaphor model we see in the example of Paul and Timothy is one possibility, and there is probably at least a little of that spiritual leadership aspect in nearly any disciple-making relationship. But beyond that, there is tremendous freedom and flexibility. In recognizing that disciple making is relational, we are simultaneously recognizing that it is personal and not formulaic, mechanistic, or industrial. Jesus' ministry was very personal and relational. It was not built on abstractions, but on interactions with real people. One of the fundamental aspects of the incarnation is that Jesus became a person, taken on flesh and blood, living within the finitude of time and space, and entering into personal relationships. Our ministries, then, ought to be personal and relational also.

There is no one single pattern for what discipleship looks like. Time, certainly, is very valuable. The relationships that involve that ingredient of time have great potential for disciple making. Invest time, particularly when given the opportunity to invest in one who is eager and ready to grow. Let go of some of the busyness of the world. Build margins in your life both for your own spiritual growth and for the opportunities of disciple making that arise. Schedule the time for disciple-making relationships. Prioritize them the way parents ought to prioritize time with their children, who are the most important disciples we are given.

That doesn't just mean formal Bible studies or that weekly coffee meeting at 3 PM on Mondays which is the scheduled "discipleship time." All of life is sacred. Every moment is opportunity for making disciples. Every word we speak, and every action that might be imitated, can be a part of that process. It may be that God gives us three or four years of regular time to invest in somebody's life on a weekly or even daily basis. Maybe like Paul and Timothy—or like most parents with their kids—we get sixteen or seventeen years. It may be that we get just one weekend a year such as I had with Eugene Peterson, and yet which made an indelible impact on my life. Or it may be what we have is an hour or two just one day on a seemingly chance meeting, and that's all. It may be that both parties are intentional. It may be that only one is.

Ultimately, disciple making is God's work. And because it is God's work, the most important thing you do in a disciple-making relationship is to pray, acknowledging our complete dependence on God.

I began this chapter suggesting that we pray to ask God what relationships he might have us invest in—even to ask God to bring people across our paths in whose lives we can work as disciple makers. But the prayer mustn't stop there. This is the final principle. I believe, also, it is the most practical.

In looking at Paul's letter to Timothy, one passage I spent little time on was the introduction to the letter. Consider the third verse of the first chapter. "I thank God, whom I serve, as my ancestors did, with a clear conscience, as night and day I constantly remember you in my prayers" (NIV). Those familiar with Paul's epistles know that this is a common refrain. Paul was committed to prayer, and in particular to personal prayers for those whose lives he worked in. As you read in the following verses, his prayers for Timothy brought to mind the particulars of Timothy's life.

Just as the transformation in our life is God's work, so to the transformation work of disciple making in the lives of others is also God's—though he grants us both the privilege and responsibility of taking part in it. So bring that work back to God repeatedly, fervently, and passionately in prayer.

Yes, disciple making is God's work, but we have a great privilege to be involved in that work with the relationships God brings across our paths.

Bibliography

Barton, Ruth Haley. *Strengthening the Soul of Your Leadership: Seeking God in the Crucible of Ministry*. Downers Grove, IL: InterVarsity, 2018.

Bono and Eugene Peterson. "Bono and Eugene Peterson: The Psalms." Directed by Nathan Clarke. Posted on YouTube April 26, 2016. www.youtube.com/watch?v=-l4oS5e9oKY.

Chi, Uli. "What Is God Like." *Life for Leaders*, January 26, 2019. lifeforleaders.depree.org/what-is-god-like.

DeYoung, Rebecca Konyndyk. "Deadly Sins and Their Remedies." Podcast with Nathan Foster, accessed 3/7/2019. renovare.org/podcast/episode-145-deadly-sins-and-their-remedies.

Dickerson, Matthew. *The Mind and the Machine: What It Means to Be Human and Why It Matters*. Eugene, OR: Cascade, 2016.

Foster, Richard. *Celebration of Discipline: The Path to Spiritual Growth*. New York: Harper and Row, 1978.

Garber, Steven. *The Fabric of Faithfulness*. Downers Grove, IL: InterVarsity, 1996.

Jacobs, Alan. *The Narnian: The Life and Imagination of C. S. Lewis*. San Francisco: Harper San Francisco, 2005.

———. "Snakes and Ladders." Blog, June 14, 2018. blog.ayjay.org/tag/evangelical/.

Johnson, Jan. *Spiritual Disciplines Companion: Bible Studies and Practices to Transform Your Soul*. Downers Grove, IL: InterVarsity, 2009.

Keyes, Dick. *Beyond Identity*. Ann Arbor, MI: Servant, 1984.

Koblin, John. "How Much Do We Love TV? Let Us Count The Ways." June 30, 2016, accessed November 15, 2018. www.nytimes.com/2016/07/01/business/media/nielsen-survey-media-viewing.html.

Lewis, C. S. *Mere Christianity*. New York: Macmillan, 1943.

Nielsen. "Time Flies: U.S. Adults Now Spend Nearly Half a Day Interacting with Media." Accessed November 15, 2018. www.nielsen.com/us/en/insights/news/2018/time-flies-us-adults-now-spend-nearly-half-a-day-interacting-with-media.html.

Peterson, Eugene. *The Jesus Way*. Grand Rapids: Eerdmans, 2007.

———. *A Long Obedience in the Same Direction*. 20th anniversary ed. Downers Grove, IL: InterVarsity, 2000.

———. *Tell It Slant*. Grand Rapids: Eerdmans, 2008.

Roberts, Mark. "Be Renewed in the Spirit of your Mind." *Life for Leaders*, March 4, 2019. lifeforleaders.depree.org/be-renewed-in-the-spirit-of-your-mind?.

Bibliography

———. "Growing Up is a Shared Experience." *Life for Leaders*, December 5, 2018. lifeforleaders.depree.org/growing-up-is-a-shared-experience.

———. "It's Not Just About You." *Life for Leaders*, December 4, 2019. lifeforleaders.depree.org/its-not-just-about-you/.

———. "You Are A Work in Progress." *Life for Leaders*, February 27, 2019. lifeforleaders.depree.org/you-are-a-work-in-progress.

Silverado. 1985, script quoted from IMDB, accessed October 15, 2019. www.imdb.com/title/tt0090022/characters/nm0000275.

Smith, Christian, and Melinda Lundquist Denton. *Soul Searching: The Religious and Spiritual Lives of American Teenagers*. New York: Oxford University Press, 2005.

Stott, John. *The Message of 2 Timothy*. Downers Grove, IL: InterVarsity, 1973.

Tolkien, J. R. R. *The Lord of the Rings*. 2d ed. Boston: Houghton Mifflin, 1966.

———. "On Fairy-Stories." In *The Monsters and the Critics, and Other Essays*, edited by Christopher Tolkien, 109–61. Boston: Houghton Mifflin, 1984.

Tripp, Paul David. *Awe: Why It Matters for Everything We Think, Say, and Do*. Wheaton, IL: Crossway, 2015.

Vine, W. E. *Vine's Expository Dictionary of New Testament Words*. Iowa Falls, IA: Riverside, 1966.

Waldman, Steven. *The Information Needs of Communities: The Changing Media Landscape in a Broadband Age*. FCC report of the working group on information needs of communities, accessed November 15, 2018. transition.fcc.gov/osp/inc-report/The_Information_Needs_of_Communities.pdf.

Wirzba, Norman. *Food and Faith: A Theology of Eating*. Cambridge: Cambridge University Press, 2011.

———. *Living the Sabbath: Discovering the Rhythms of Rest and Delight*. Grand Rapids: Brazos, 2006.

www.ingramcontent.com/pod-product-compliance
Lightning Source LLC
Chambersburg PA
CBHW031503160426
43195CB00010BB/1093